RESILIENCE FOR FILMMAKERS, CREATIVES & SOLO CREATORS

STAYING LIT WHEN THE WORLD SAYS QUIT

LANTERN LEARNINGS

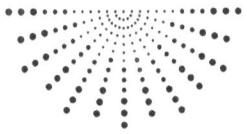

NIKHIL KAMKOLKAR

RESILIENCE FOR FILMMAKERS, CREATIVES & SOLO CREATORS
Staying Lit When the World Says Quit

Nikhil Kamkolkar

To report errors, please send a note to lanternlearnings@gmail.com

KAMKOL
Kamkol titles may be purchased in bulk for educational, business, promotional or training use. Inquiries should be addressed to nikhil@kamkol.com

Identifiers
ISBN 978-1-970338-00-3 (paperback)
ISBN 978-1-970338-02-7 (hardcover)

For my Mom & Dad
who are watching
all my wins
all my losses
all my struggles
from up above
with the total and complete belief that
I
will
achieve
what
I
want...
reminding me
that
resilience
often
needs
faith...

CONTENTS

ACT II

WHY DO YOU WANT RESILIENCE?

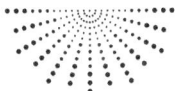

*I*t'd be so much easier to quit.

I've sat in the dark, staring at my work—at the polished bio that can feel like a beggar in a suit—and wondered if I'll ever truly make it as a filmmaker. The truth is that behind every polished bio lies a shadow story: innumerable rejections, abandoned projects, compromises made for survival, and the endless tension between art and livelihood

And yet, something keeps me going.

Resilience.

From the Latin *resilire*—*re* ("again/back") and *salire* ("to leap")—resilience means to spring back after being pushed away.

In a creative life, it's as essential as craft—and luck.

WHAT THIS BOOK IS—AND ISN'T

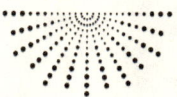

This book is a field guide to the human side of creative work —inner life and community, collaboration and conflict, boundaries and openness, resilience and recovery. It offers **Lantern Learnings™**—practical principles and small, repeatable practices you can use today to keep creating, even when recognition lags and the industry wobbles.

It isn't a craft manual on how to shoot a film or write a script. It isn't a handbook for "making it" in the industry. It's something simpler: a way to stay lit when everything around you pressures you to quit.

Think of a lantern. It doesn't flood the horizon with light; it gives just enough for the next step. These pages don't promise riches or recognition. They offer guidance forged in the in-between: working day jobs to support the work, relearning my craft in a world remade by AI, and honoring the demands of my art alongside family responsibilities.

If you're here, you may be carrying questions: How do I balance the dream with the grind? How do I survive the demands of a creative practice when recognition feels so far away? How do I honor my loved ones while honoring my calling? How do I keep going?

My answer isn't a glossy roadmap; it's a lantern. It won't banish the dark, but it may give you a glimmer of insight to help you keep walking—and notice, then strengthen, the invisible threads of resilience that steady you when the path turns uncertain.

WHO THIS BOOK IS FOR

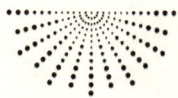

I am a writer–filmmaker–actor. This multihyphenate life has taught me a simple truth: The struggles in these pages belong to anyone trying to create—writers, painters, designers, musicians, performers. The details differ; the struggle is shared.

Before you go further, pause and write one sentence: "I got this book so I can ___."

Don't overthink it. As you read this book, you can return to that line often and see how it shifts.

Now, sit with this question: Why do I want resilience?

- To finish what I start?
- To provide for my family?
- To see my stories or my art reach the screen, stage, concert hall, or gallery?
- To prove something—to myself or to others?
- To keep the flame alive for one more season, one last push?

AFTER YOU READ THIS CHAPTER, I want you to write a short paragraph —just for you. Let it be raw, jagged, even contradictory. Then ask again: Why does this matter to me? Keep peeling back with "Why?" until you touch something steady, even if small.

That is the resilience that can support you in your life.

Here's an example of how I did this for a recent decision I faced around creating an anthology of my short films. There were many reasons to not do it. I'd be spending time on older material, instead of creating a new film. The material itself would be frustrating to work with as it'd reflect the limitations on both talent, craft, and resources I was able to bring to bear on it. It also risked putting work out there that may undersell my current abilities and level of craft.

I decided to not do it.

But my intuition wouldn't give up badgering me. So I did a timed writing for an hour, asking the question why and answering it. Over and over. Here's a sample of how some of that non-stop writing and wrestling with myself asking "why should I make this anthology" looked like:

Why do I want to revisit my short films? Why not work on the new feature project I've committed to deliver? I want to do this to respect the work everyone else had put into the short film projects. Why do you have to do that? They did the films. They are not asking about it. Well, I want to build my completion muscle. Good, bad or ugly, I want to complete the films and for me, completion means distribution. Why not just put them online? Yes. I could do that. But I feel like that's not a good experience for the audience. Why not? The films by themselves are not enough of a value proposition, but together, they work thematically and offer more value. So what? A new film you make can also offer value. Why go back to the older films? Because I made mistakes. And if I don't fully recognize what they were, and understand them deeply, I will just make the same mistakes again on the new film. Why not make them on the new film? Because the stakes are higher, much higher. With these short films, the learnings will not cost me much beyond some amount of time. It'll also exercise all the training I've undergone, especially with regard to Color Correction, and post-production in general. By learning what the mistakes on set mean in post, I can then ensure I don't make those on my next film. But why not? You'll make new mistakes anyway. Yes, but they won't be rookie mistakes. I'll understand how my storytelling didn't communicate effortlessly in a eight minute short film. I'll test it with my fellow filmmakers. I'll learn and apply those to my feature. Plus, I can develop workflows in both post and on-set production that will help me make the next film faster and better...

And that went on for quite a bit. By putting this debate down on paper in a timed writing (where I write continuously for a set amount of time without stopping at all, even if that means I scribble circles on the page), what I walked away at the end of it were very practical reasons to make the anthology.

1. By making the anthology, I'd help myself build an architecture in terms of workflows and infrastructure to help make my next film feasible, and perhaps even succeed in the marketplace.
2. By making the anthology, I'd clear a debt I was carrying around in my mind of all these short films that remained unreleased.
3. By making the anthology, I'd test out the entire post-production pipeline I have been learning. Editing, audio post, grading, and creating Netflix-quality deliverables.
4. By making the anthology, I'd strengthen my storytelling skills and put all the techniques I've been studying for the past six years into practice. It'd help me to use them effectively in my next project.

NOW IT'S YOUR TURN. Write your own paragraph. Keep asking yourself: Why?

HOW TO USE THIS BOOK

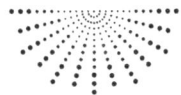

*T*his is not a book you read once and shelve. It's a field guide.

Each Lantern Learning follows the same shape:

First an investigation that provides context and a close look at the idea.

Followed by:

Principle—the distilled insight

Then, Practice and/or Reflection—small actions to try, or questions to journal on.

You can move through the book in either of two ways:

Straight Through—follow the arc of Becoming, Belonging, and Evolving as a narrative of growth.

Dip In—open the book to any Lantern Learning when you're stuck, tired, or in doubt.

Some days you'll want reflection. Other days you'll want action. This book is meant for both.

A few tips to get the most from it:

Keep it close. Leave it on your desk or carry it in your bag. It's designed for rereading in small doses. Write in it too.

Mark your light. Highlight or dog-ear the Lanterns that hit strongest. Return to them when the flame feels faint.

One practice at a time. Don't do them all at once. Repeat one until it becomes part of your rhythm.

Return when you falter. This isn't about mastering every lesson; it's about having a place to come back to.

This book offers no roadmap and no false guarantees.

It offers a lantern—just enough light for the next step.

ACT I

BECOMING

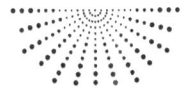

THE PATH OF BECOMING

*B*eing an artist isn't only about the work. It's about moving through careers and relationships that are messy, asymmetrical, and demanding. Without clarity about your inner drivers and principles, you get swept into others' urgencies, expectations, and entitlements.

Clarity of self is the foundation.

Before you step into the world, know what you stand on.

Becoming isn't arriving fully formed. It's stabilizing yourself so you can show up, compass in hand, and walk into uncertainty with strength.

Grace is the ground you stand on.

It's your inner orientation. It steadies you. With grace, you move without panic and rest without apology. Without it, you spiral.

Presence is showing up fully

Presence begins by literally grounding yourself. Everyone finds their own method. I do it by standing up, my weight evenly balanced on my feet. Then I start by feeling every part of my foot on the ground as I tread and roll each foot. Then I work my way up my body, rolling every joint, making myself aware of every part of my body, and releasing any tension held anywhere. This is too brief an explanation for what you may need to ground yourself, but look up bodywork techniques and try out a few. I recommend Rie Katagiri, a movement coach based in Los Angeles who offers classes online.

Once grounded, practice presence. Be here, engaged, awake to the moment. This is not about performance. It's about total availability. People feel it when you're present. They feel it when you're not.

Role is your function within a context

Grace + presence brings your role into focus. Your role is situational: in this room, at this moment, you serve in this way. It is not your identity. It is how you become useful at this exact time.

Purpose & Alignment is the why behind the role. A role without purpose is mechanical. Purpose tethers what you do to what matters. It answers the question: Why does this matter—for me and for those I serve? Even small tasks gain strength when linked to purpose.

Lift your eyes to your guiding star. It's not a finish line; it offers coherence and gives you a direction to set out toward. Your true north already exists within you; you reveal it to yourself over time.

But knowing your purpose isn't enough. You need to be able to determine if any given request aligns with it. Does this work match my values? Am I moving in the direction I intend? This is not about perfection—you'll always stray off the path. This is about constant course correction.

Impact is proof of your contribution to the world

Purpose is aspirational until it's tested. Impact is the evidence of what holds, what resonates, what changes—the laboratory of Becoming.

Impact brings feedback. Course correction or steadiness is your response.

In sum, this is the sequence line of Becoming:

Grace → Presence → Role → Purpose & Alignment → Impact

You won't follow this in order every time, but you will touch every aspect as you come into your own resilience.

At the end of BECOMING, you're not "done." You're calibrated: rooted in grace, steady in presence, clear on role, animated by purpose and corrected by alignment, and driven by impact.

That is enough to begin—and enough to iterate for life.

Why This Matters to Resilience

Resilience needs a shape to spring back to. Without Becoming, there's no "you" to return to—only drift.

Difficulty will still come—doubt, rejection, scarcity, fatigue. Becoming gives you the contours to come back to.

Resilience isn't just endurance; it's the capacity to return, again and again, to the path you chose.

Simple to say, but rarely easy.

Practice

On an index card, write the sequence line.

Grace → Presence → Role → Purpose & Alignment → Impact

Under it, jot one word for where you feel most available today (e.g., "Grace"). Keep it in your wallet. Walk through the world knowing you are holding Grace as your guide.

On the other hand, if you are feeling flustered and off-balance, and you have a meeting or a shoot coming up, then try doing this. Breathe calmly for three cycles and silently state: Grace (I'm steady), Presence (I'm here), Role (I'm here to ___), Purpose (so that ___). Sometimes the very act of naming your guides can help calm down your nervous system.

At day's end, write one sentence answering this question: Did I move toward alignment with my purpose? If yes, what was it? If not, what one aspect can I investigate tomorrow? There is no pass or fail here. Just a constant desire to improve your alignment with every new moment.

2

GRACE

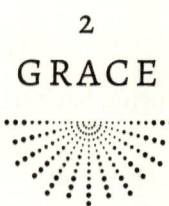

*E*very creative journey begins not with the world but with yourself. Your inner orientation is the soil from which every choice grows—how you treat yourself, how you treat others, how you carry the inevitable burdens of making work that matters.

Some begin with discipline. Some with ambition. Some with sheer survival. If you want your light to last, let it begin with grace. Grace is not softness or indulgence. It is the clear decision to meet yourself and others with generosity before judgment, with care before punishment.

Grace is not infinite. It requires boundaries. With them, grace steadies both the solitary walk of the artist and the unruly economy of community.

Here is the hinge to resilience: Resilience is the capacity to return; grace is the stance that lets you return without breaking. Resilience pulls you back to the path. Grace gives you the strength—and the shape—to come back intact.

In this part, we practice grace in layers: first for the self, then within limits, then as a freely chosen gift; we right-size it to each situation, carry it in public as silence and signal, and temper it with discernment.

This section asks a simple question with practical edges: What does it look like to move through the world with grace?

3

GRACE FOR SELF

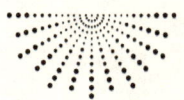

*L*et's get something straight.

Sometimes, the most radical grace is for yourself. Sometimes, blindly following your stated principles with no regard for anything else, may not be the best thing to do.

Yes, even the principles I'm presenting in this book.

The purpose of these lantern principles is not to trap you in them, but to give you language for feelings you may not have spoken yet. To help you recognize patterns in yourself and others. To hold a mirror to your inner life you already know but haven't named.

These lantern principles are not commandments. They are language, not law. They help you name what you feel, not dictate what you must do.

You are not bound to always shine. You can cover the lantern, dim the flame, or act without explanation. You are not required to live by principles every moment of every day.

There will be times when what you must do doesn't align neatly with grace, clarity, or fit. Times when survival, instinct, or urgency demands a choice outside of principle. That is not failure. That is free will.

Use the lantern when it helps you see. Ignore it when it doesn't.

Your agency, your choice, your inner compass—these are greater than any book or set of words.

The lantern is here to walk beside you, not command your steps.

Principle

Principles are guides, not cages; your agency comes first.

Practice

Write a permission slip: "I may dim the lantern when survival or sanity or kindness requires it."

Exception log: Note one time you chose outside the principle and why.

For instance, my most recent exception to the lantern idea of sticking to my boundary was when someone asked me for a favor. I knew I could say no. But I felt the need for a kinder response and said yes. But I did it with fullness of presence and was therefore not frustrated by my choice.

4
GRACE WITHIN LIMITS

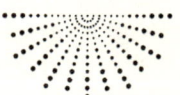

The creative world we move in is its own small economy. We trade support, attention, and energy—not just money. Perhaps we are more like beggars with pride rather than royalty—seeking to be seen, to have our work valued, to keep creating. Stardom is rare; the struggle is constant.

The only sustainable path through it all is grace. Grace toward others: meeting their efforts with generosity, even when it's small. Grace toward self: giving time, care, and energy to your own work without self-punishment.

Grace, generosity, and the choice to start from care rather than punishment shape the kind of lantern you carry. Your nature is the key. Make grace the foundation—your beginning stance toward yourself, your peers, and the long road ahead.

But generosity is not infinite. True grace requires boundaries. Without them, generosity burns itself out. A lantern cannot light the path for others if it consumes its own flame.

PRINCIPLE

Grace sustains; boundaries protect.

PRACTICE

Audit your flame: List three things you gave away this week. Note what drained you.

Set one boundary: Say a kind, firm no to one request.

Give with intention: Choose one act of generosity that energizes you.

5

GRACE GIVEN FREELY

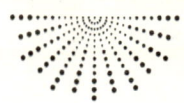

Generosity is only grace if it's given freely. The moment it becomes a debt, a duty, or a way to prevent abandonment, it loses its light.

There's a difference between choosing to give and being cornered into giving. The first sustains you. The second drains you. When you are drained, anger is natural—anger at them for taking, and anger at yourself for allowing it.

The lantern way is this: Give when it strengthens you, not when it empties you. A yes that costs your peace is too expensive. A no that protects your light isn't selfish—it's necessary.

Grace is a gift, not a currency. The moment it feels transactional, step back. The lantern shines because it burns steadily, not because it gives its flame to every hand that reaches in.

PRINCIPLE

Grace is chosen, not coerced; a yes that costs your peace is too expensive.

PRACTICE

Motivation check: Before you say *yes*, ask, "Am I giving freely or from fear/obligation?"

Use a pause: If you feel cornered, wait before replying.

Keep a "kind no" ready: "Thanks for thinking of me, but I can't take this on."

6

GRADATIONS OF GRACE

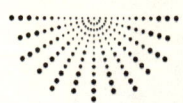

*N*ot every relationship deserves the same depth of response. Some require full presence; some need only a nod. Grace isn't all-or-nothing—it's proportion. Protect your nervous system by offering the right layer of grace for the situation.

PRINCIPLE

Grace can be cordial without being costly.

PRACTICE

Before responding, ask: What's the smallest kind of grace this situation truly needs? Offer only that.

7

GRACE OF RESTRAINT

*G*race is also how you carry yourself in public. In a culture that rewards volume, grace chooses restraint. In a market addicted to headlines, grace chooses focus. The rhythm of silence preserves your energy for the work; resonance lets the work speak.

Silence can be power. Audiences don't care about laurels or bios. They care about stories that move them. Substance is the only currency that endures when the noise fades.

Noise is easy to mistake for progress—announcements, accolades, posts. It creates the illusion of momentum and burns energy without depth.

What matters is resonance—the part of your work that lingers after the tab closes. Even a 2–5% response—a handful of people deeply moved—is proof. The real measure is whether someone who has never heard your name can sit with your work and feel something.

Make rhythm and consistency your strength. A steady lantern outlasts fireworks.

PRINCIPLE

Noise fades; resonance lasts.

PRACTICE

Make the work the headline: Ship one finishable piece this month.

One piece, five strangers: Plan for five strangers to encounter your work without you present.

Skip one shout: Hold back an announcement; let the work speak.

Track resonance: Log after-effects (callbacks, shares, repeat views).

Build rhythm: Choose a small, repeatable release cadence (weekly sketch/monthly short).

GRACE WITH DISCERNMENT

*P*eople are human. We all have good days, bad days, blind spots, defenses. Sometimes, to protect themselves, they recast you as the problem. That doesn't make them villains. It makes them human.

The trap is treating human imperfection as acceptable partnership.

Grace says: Don't demonize.

Discernment says: Don't ignore red flags.

Hold both at the same time.

PRINCIPLE

Grace without discernment is naivety. Discernment without grace is hostility. Together, they keep you steady.

PRACTICE

Catch yourself when you start to demonize someone else. Journal your thoughts as you attempt to discern the truth from your judgment. This is an exercise in "seeing things as they are" and not "as you think they are."

CASE STUDY: DOWNEY & FAVREAU

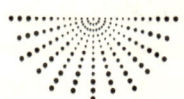

*E*arly 2000s.

Robert Downey Jr. was a cautionary tale—addiction, arrests, and an "uninsurable" label that made studios look away. Yet he kept showing up, rebuilding his sobriety, and doing the work.

At the same time, Marvel, not the powerful studio it is now, was financing its own films. *Iron Man* wasn't a sure thing, and a fail with that project could end the company. The last thing the executives wanted was a risky lead.

But the director Jon Favreau saw something special in Downey: alignment with the character of Tony Stark. Robert Downey Jr. was a brilliant man who had nearly lost himself and fought his way back. Downey had essentially lived out Tony Stark's arc!

Favreau advocated for Downey, but with the support of evidence. Recent acting showed Downey reliable—prepared, present, hungry. And he was the perfect fit for the role. Downey's charisma wasn't cosmetic—it was character.

That alone wasn't enough. Insurance, accountability, and a production plan were put in place to protect the film if Downey self-destructed.

This wasn't blanket forgiveness. It was grace with discernment, with responsible guardrails put in place to protect the project and the studio. Downey didn't just deliver—he defined the role. The film was a hit, to put it mildly, and the studio's future changed course.

TAKEAWAYS

Don't excuse but assess. Look for evidence of change. Don't rely on promises.

Discern when the story meets an actor's lived experience, because that kind of alignment amplifies performance.

Extend grace, but with guardrails (insurance, accountability, contingency). Protect the work *and* the person.

Hold different standards. A family may weather fights and continue, but professional ties don't require that level of tolerance. One red flag can be enough.

Discernment says *when* to say yes; boundaries shape *how*.

Sometimes—with evidence and with structure—you can stand beside someone as they change. Other times the right choice is letting go.

PRINCIPLE

Grace humanizes; discernment protects.

PRACTICE

Notice what an event (insult, rejection, etc.) triggers within you and name the feelings (disappointment, betrayal) so neither the event nor your feelings define you.

Humanize. Decide they're human, not villains. Then ask, does this relationship serve the work? If not, end it cleanly.

GRACE AS FOUNDATION

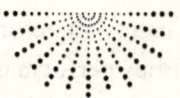

*W*ithout grace, resilience can harden into bitterness. With grace, resilience becomes sustainable. You can return to the path without breaking yourself in the process.

PRESENCE

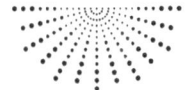

*P*resence is how you show up. It's the foundation beneath every other pillar of Becoming. Before you define your role, name your purpose, or measure your impact, be present, fully attentive, and ready to serve the work in front of you with grace.

Presence isn't about titles or outcomes. It's the quality of your attention and the steadiness of your state—the readiness to contribute with ease.

At its simplest, presence is attention. What you notice—and what you feed with your energy—becomes your reality. Guard your bandwidth; let go of loops that don't serve the work.

Presence doesn't require overpreparation. You don't need to predict every turn; you need to steady yourself. Let your response be grounded and measured.

Presence rejects perfectionism. It works with what's here. It asks not for polish, but for availability—to listen, to adjust, to make a useful contribution when the moment calls. It also needs enough inner quiet to sense the next move—and the freedom to let it be small.

When you strip away the noise, presence is simple:

Guard your attention.

Steady your state.

Be available to the moment.

Offer the next useful contribution when it's time.

Resilience without presence is brittle—chasing outcomes, being tethered to what others think.

With presence, resilience is fluid. You can be knocked down and still reenter the moment—go back to the breath, the page, the shot, the scene—ready to contribute again.

12

START WITH ATTENTION

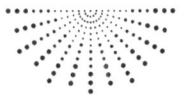

*P*resence begins with attention. What you feed with your focus becomes your state.

Comparison loops, replayed arguments, distressing interactions—these are unpaid tenants in the mental space you need for craft and peace.

Evict them.

Protect the bandwidth that you need to meet your priorities fluidly, fully, and meaningfully in the moment.

This isn't indifference; it's respect for your instrument. It's radical focus. As Indian actor-producer Shah Rukh Khan—one of the world's most-watched film stars—has said in interviews, he doesn't spend time thinking about people, good or bad. His attention is reserved for his family and for his work. That refusal to host others "rent-free" in his head preserves mental energy for what truly matters to him—his work and the people he cares about.

PRINCIPLE

What you attend to becomes your state. Guard your attention so you're ready to make the next useful contribution.

PRACTICE

Single-point return: Create your own tiny anchor of physical behavior (three deep breaths, writing one line on the page) that you return to when you notice your attention drifting.

After-contact protocol: Give full attention in the moment; when it ends, take one clearing breath, label any replay "entanglement," and return to your anchor.

Attention audit (weekly): List your top three recurring loops. Circle the one that you feel is important for you to act on; retire the others.

Address red flags early: If a lingering doubt or a misfit partner keeps draining you, turn it into one decisive step (clarify, renegotiate, or exit).

REFLECTION

Attention is preparation. When you keep the lane clear, your contribution lands cleanly—on the page, the shot, the scene.

PHYSICAL PRESENCE

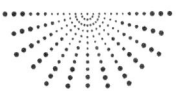

*W*ith family, with relationships, with art, sometimes what matters most is not what you do but that you are there—present, open, unhurried.

When I said no to an ask from a colleague, I found myself able to say yes to something priceless: an hour and a half at my kid's soccer practice. Nothing "productive" happened. I watched, asked questions, saw details I would've missed. That's not a transaction; that's presence.

Availability is the soil where happy accidents, small surprises, and deep memories take root. If you treat your availability for your loved ones like a task, they'll always lose to the next urgent work thing. Offer your unhurried and total availability and you give them—and yourself—the chance to be surprised by what unfolds.

PRINCIPLE

Availability isn't wasted time. It is presence without agenda.

PRACTICE

Protect open hours. Leave space in your schedule not just for work, but for being with those who matter—without agenda.

Reclaim availability. Notice where you've given your time away (calls, obligations, distractions), and consider whether it belongs back with your family, your art, or yourself.

Celebrate the unplanned. When nothing "happens" in that available time, don't call it wasted. Presence is the point.

Anchor in memory. After moments of pure availability, jot down what you noticed or felt. Don't put the pressure on the moment for "what came out of it"—that's not the point at all.

ENTANGLEMENT

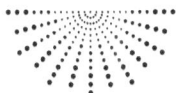

*P*resence is fuel.

When you're with someone—a loved one, a colleague, even a neighbor at a party—let them feel you are truly there. For those minutes, give them your full beam. When the moment ends, don't carry home their judgments, their expectations, or their disappointments as if they belong to you.

This is the art of warmth without weight.

This way, you shine fully in the moment, but you do not drag the moment along with you.

PRINCIPLE

True presence gives light without entanglement.

PRACTICE

1. Full signal: In each encounter, silence the inner commentary. Let the other person feel you are there.

2. Cut the carry: Afterward, write down one insight or kindness from the exchange. Release the rest.
3. Return to center: Re-anchor on your role: What craft or care needs your attention now?

15

PRESENCE WITHOUT PANIC

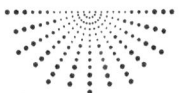

*T*he gap between projects can rattle your nerves. When nothing active is on your plate, the urge is to prove you're still here—posting to feel relevant, making things just to share. You don't have to do that. You can choose how you show up in the in-between so you stay ready without burning fuel.

PRINCIPLE

Be ready, not busy. Soothe the nervous system, protect the craft, and choose your mode on purpose.

You can be a builder who goes completely silent in-between projects. You can be someone who delivers a steady pulse to the world without turning it into a full-time job. Or you can share everything you experience during the gap. Whatever you do, don't do it to self-soothe. Do it intentionally.

PRACTICE

Reset on purpose: Schedule two unhurried blocks for rest or time with your people.

Keep the craft warm: Spend 10 minutes a day on your instrument (whatever that might be).

Start the next thing: Take one concrete step (a one-page brief, one email, reach out to one scout).

Write the next step: For each project, note the single next action so you can avoid mental loops.

Simple check-in (weekly): Did my choice of mode leave me more ready or more exhausted?

WHAT TO AVOID

Posting to calm panic.

Starting five new things at once.

Making content only to fill the quiet.

Watching metrics instead of making progress.

REFLECTION

In the interval between projects, be the pilot light—low and steady. What do you think of that approach? Do you think that by doing it this way, when the next project lands, you will ignite fast with no wasted time and lots of conserved energy?

1 6

ROLE

*P*resence gathers your light. Role gives it a frame.

Walk into a room without a compass and people will project their needs onto you—"the Unreal Engine person," "the tech guy," "the sound guy." Your story will dissolve into theirs. Define your role and frame it with intention, and you give the world a clear way to meet you.

This isn't optics; it's survival. A scattered reel, a half-finished site, a vague answer to "What do you do?"—these blur your light. A clear role, shown consistently through your work, gives clarity to others and helps them understand what you do.

This part is about three moves: define your lane, say it cleanly, and make the frame match.

CLARITY FIRST

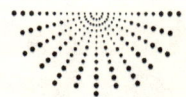

*Y*ou can't move with confidence if you don't know your lane. In creative work, motion without clarity may look like progress, but it's drift.

When you chase opportunities before defining your role, you risk getting miscast. You stay busy but not aligned with your goals; you move, but are not advancing.

Clarity is knowing who you are in the room and why you're there.

It's a single phrase role. It's not a résumé. It's more of a presence. For example: I am a filmmaker, storyteller, educator and I work at the intersection of storytelling, cinema, and technology.

When you have clarity, others know how to approach you, and you know when to step forward or step back.

PRINCIPLE

Clarity before motion.

The clarity test:

Can you describe what you do in one or two sentences?

Can you say why this matters—to you, and to others?

Can you show how today's work connects to your body of work?

If not, pause. Define before you move. This pause will save more time than it costs.

PRACTICE

Write your two-sentence role (what you do + how you do it differently).

Anchor the why (who it serves and why it matters).

Link the work (tie today's task to your body of work).

Use it consistently (bios, intros, panels, conversations).

Mirror check (Do your public artifacts match the role you claim?).

18

YOUR FRAME

*H*ow people see you is shaped not just by who you are, but by the frame around you. If your panels, reels, shorts, or courses are half-finished, the world reads you as scattered.

Even great work can fade without focus. But when the frame is intentional, the picture comes into focus. A clear website, a curated reel, a polished short—these aren't vanity pieces. They're the edges that center and reveal your core.

PRINCIPLE

A strong frame reveals the picture you want the world to see.

PRACTICE

Curate, don't dump: Pick the 2–3 best artifacts (shorts, essays, reels).

Tighten one edge: Update one outward-facing platform to reflect your role.

Align the language: Make sure your two-sentence role appears everywhere people meet you—from social media, to LinkedIn, to in-person introductions

Run a consistency audit: Do your words + artifacts tell one unified and coherent story?

19

CURATE WHERE YOU SHOW UP

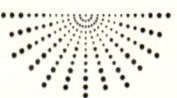

 ou don't need to be everywhere. You need to be in the right spaces—often enough that your presence feels intentional.

THE COST OF BEING EVERYWHERE

Chasing every speaking panel, festival, or networking space scatters your energy. It spreads you thin, has you showing up half-prepared, and puts you in rooms that don't matter to your work. This doesn't build trust and it leads to fatigue.

THE POWER OF BEING IN THE RIGHT SPACE

When you show up where your craft belongs, you become recognizable. Over time, people begin to expect your voice, your work, your perspective. It's not about volume; it's about rhythm and context. A consistent presence in the right spaces makes you memorable.

How to Curate Where You Show Up

• Ask: Does this space align with my role and frame?

    • Prioritize spaces where your true audience or peers gather.

    • Return consistently so your presence becomes part of the landscape.

A lantern doesn't light every corner of the dark. It makes its chosen space visible. Curate where you show up, and you'll create not just visibility but belonging.

Principle

Curate the spaces where you show up.

Practice

Do an audit: List five spaces you showed up in recently. Did they serve your intention?

Choose two: Pick your two most aligned communities and return regularly.

Exit one: Drop at least one space that drains more than it gives.

PURPOSE AND ALIGNMENT

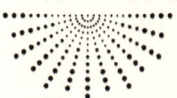

*P*urpose is both direction and filter—less a slogan than a tool for choosing what gets a yes and what gets a no. It sets the direction of your effort.

Alignment is fit: your hours, outputs, and public story match your stated purpose. Together, purpose points your energy; alignment keeps you honest and steady once you commit. That steadiness is resilience in practice.

Presence readies you. Role frames you. Purpose chooses the way. Alignment holds you to it.

PURPOSE OVER AVAILABILITY

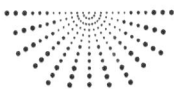

*L*et others choose you for alignment, not availability. Being available isn't the same as being a fit.

THE TRAP

Say yes because you feel flattered, needed, or included and you'll end up with work that doesn't honor your purpose.

THE POINT OF ALIGNMENT

When your craft and purpose align, your yes means something, and people trust it.

THE PURPOSE TEST

Does this align with my craft and lane?
 Does it serve my growth or my audience's experience?
 Does it protect my peace and honor my principles?
 Will I be proud to have my name on this?

PRINCIPLE

Availability is convenient; alignment earns trust.

PRACTICE

Pause before saying yes to an ask; don't reply in the moment.

Run the purpose test.

When the work doesn't fit with your purpose, decline simply with grace: "Thanks for thinking of me, but I can't take this on."

Develop and share a short public role statement so people know when you're the right call—and when you're not.

Example — Using Ikigai to Shape a LinkedIn Summary

I revisit my LinkedIn summary whenever my interests, capabilities, or the market shifts. The concept of Ikigai is the filter: Does this reflect the overlap of what I love, what I'm good at, what people need, and what pays?

Current Summary

I'm a writer-filmmaker and Unreal Authorized Instructor (Gold), crafting stories powered by real-time engines, virtual production, and AI tools. My focus? Bridging creative vision with tech innovation—whether in indie features like LOVE LOVE (now on Amazon), award-winning shorts, or coursework in mocap and Unreal Metahumans.

PURPOSE OVER URGENCY

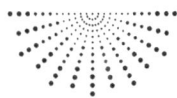

*N*ot every ask deserves speed.

Urgency without alignment can often turn their problem into your emergency, forcing you to skip your filter and say yes when you should have said no.

Let alignment set the pace. If the work fits your craft and purpose, honor urgency. If it doesn't, speed doesn't matter. You're sprinting down a road that isn't yours.

THE ALIGNMENT–URGENCY GRID

Aligned + urgent = ACT

These are rare moments worth dropping everything for.

Aligned + not urgent = SCHEDULE

These build steady momentum.

Not aligned + urgent = DECLINE

This is someone else's fire, not yours.

Not aligned + not urgent = IGNORE

Not your circus, not your monkeys. Ignore it and don't let it rent space in your mind.

PRINCIPLE

Purpose before pace; let urgency follow alignment.

PRACTICE

Name the clock: When a "rush" arrives, ask, Whose deadline is this?
Run the grid: ACT / SCHEDULE / DECLINE / IGNORE.
Buy the pause: "I'll review and get back to you by [time]."
Guard the boundary: "I can't take this on under these timelines."
Track false alarms: Note one "urgent" thing you delayed that didn't matter. Train the instinct.
Pre-commit windows: Reserve time for aligned work so true urgencies have somewhere to land.

PURPOSE STEADIES YOUR FLAME

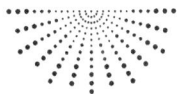

*B*eware the flattering ask, the thrill of being needed, the adrenaline of someone else's urgency. If your light bends to every wind, it burns out.

Purpose isn't saying yes more often; it's saying yes with clarity. Step in when the work matches your flame. Step away when it does not.

24

IMPACT

*I*mpact is what remains after you release the work—what resonates, returns, and ripples.

Applause is loud and fleeting. Impact is quieter, and it compounds. Finish, deliver on time, then measure what comes back.

25

COMPLETION CURRENCY

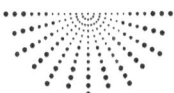

*I*n a noisy market, partial progress doesn't register. What earns trust, collaborators, and future work is finished work at a credible—and ideally, impressive—standard.

PRINCIPLE

Completion leads to future work.

PRACTICE

Release finished pieces publicly (even modest ones) so they circulate.

Skip filler social media posting: Don't post just to soothe your nervous system or chase a dopamine hit. Save your energy for substance.

Let finished work, delivered on a cadence, make the case for your capabilities.

REFLECTION

In an era where everyone announces, completion is the rarest flex—
the currency that reliably turns into future work.

26

DELIVER THE PERFORMANCE

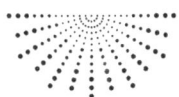

Opportunities don't end when the door opens; they begin there. A first call becomes the last call if you don't deliver. Performance isn't perfection; it's reliability.

A lantern isn't measured by how many times it's lit, but by how reliably it shines once it's burning. Deliver the performance on time and with quality, and people will return to your light.

PRINCIPLE

Opportunities begin after the door opens. Consistency keeps the door open.

PRACTICE

Prepare beyond minimum: Treat each shot like it might be the only one.

Bring steadiness: Be on time, organized, calm. Make reliability part of the craft.

Set and meet expectations: State clearly what you'll deliver and when.

Close with care: Send crisp follow-ups (notes, links, next steps, timelines).

Debrief: Note for yourself what worked, what slipped, and capture your learnings.

27

MEASURE PROOF
THROUGH IMPACT

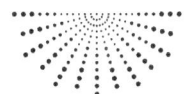

*P*roof isn't the headlines; it's the aftermath—what happens after all the applause and headlines are in the rearview mirror.

Impact keeps your lantern shining in the dark long after the noise has died down.

PRINCIPLE

Measure the impact of your work landing in the world, not the decibel level of the announcements.

PRACTICE

Track the impact: Callbacks, referrals, repeat views/hires.

Reframe success: Log outcomes (second meetings, reuse, trust earned).

Build for return: Give each piece a next step (watch, reply, share, book).

Ask for resonance: Invite one viewer to say what stayed with them; capture their language.

Monthly impact audit: Spend ten minutes figuring out which work actually had an impact.

BECOME A STEADY LIGHT

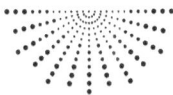

*W*ork alone isn't enough. It must be seen, remembered, and trusted—and that comes from coherence.

Grace steadies. Presence readies. Role frames. Purpose chooses. Alignment holds. Impact proves.

When these line up, your light is steady.

29

INTERLUDE: FAKE IT
TILL YOU MAKE IT?

In creative circles, "fake it till you make it" gets repeated like gospel. At its best, it's a strategy for resilience: When you feel uncertain inside, you practice steadiness on the outside. You act as though you belong until the belonging starts to feel real.

But there's a shadow side. Faking too long can slip into armor—building an identity that looks solid to others but feels hollow to you. If resilience is the capacity to return to your path, armor can become the weight that keeps you off it.

The truth is, everyone fakes it sometimes. The leap into a new role, the first panel, the first time you're called "director" or "DP" or "author." Resilience in these moments isn't about denying the gap between who you are and who you're becoming. It's about walking that gap with honesty—knowing you're still learning, still becoming, but choosing to step forward anyway.

The trick is to treat "faking it" not as deception, but as rehearsal. You step into the role to grow into it. But you don't stay in the mask. You shed the armor as soon as you can stand steady without it.

Resilience isn't pretending forever. It's holding yourself through the awkward middle—long enough for the outside performance and the inside truth to finally align.

ACT II

BELONGING

*I*f BECOMING gave you the foundation—clarity about who you are and what you stand for—BELONGING is where that clarity gets tested.

The truth is that you don't live in isolation. You live—and create—in a world of collaborators, communities, and shifting alliances. Resilience here isn't just inner grit; it's staying steady when other people pull, push, or disappoint.

Belonging isn't fitting in at any cost. It's knowing when to join, when to walk away, and how to carry yourself without dimming your flame.

This act gives you practical frames for partnerships, communities, boundaries, voice, and endings—so you can protect integrity and still honor connection.

It's rarely clean. And often awkward. But this is where you learn which people and places let your work thrive, or not.

Becoming steadies the flame; Belonging is carrying it among others without letting it bend.

31
SELF-ALIGNMENT

Start on the inside. If you don't belong to your own principles, any circle can own you. Here we'll sort **true belonging** from **conditional acceptance**, practice **saying no without drama**, write **non-negotiables**, and learn **when to repair vs. when to exit**.

Use the reflections to check your alignment; use the practice tips to act. The goal isn't isolation. It's choosing communities where your work and your boundaries are both welcome.

32

BELONGING WITHOUT BENDING

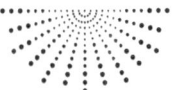

The nervous system treats belonging as survival. Thousands of years ago, being cast out of the pack meant death. That wiring hasn't changed. When someone ignores you, withdraws friendship, or shuts a door, your body might react as if your life is in danger—shutting down focus, especially in creative work.

This survival-level need for belonging collides with the reality of a solitary craft. Filmmaking, writing, and creating often demand long stretches of aloneness. That can feel like exile, even when it's chosen. The tension is real: Your art asks you to stand apart, while your body begs to stay in the pack.

The lantern way is to recognize both truths. You do need touch-points of belonging—but you don't have to bend yourself to fit noisy circles or conditional friendships. A pack doesn't have to be hundreds of peers or a buzzing community. It can be a handful of steady people, or even the rhythm of your own craft, reminding you that you are not alone.

The test isn't "Am I accepted everywhere?" but "Do I have enough anchors to keep my nervous system steady?" Don't bend yourself just to be chosen. Build bonds—even small ones—that let your nervous system rest and your lantern stay lit.

PRINCIPLE

Belonging steadies the nervous system; build anchors (see practice below) so you don't bend to be chosen.

PRACTICE

Name the alarm: When exclusion hits, say to yourself: "This is my nervous system thinking I'm unsafe. But I am safe." Naming the trigger takes away its false authority.

Anchor physically: Walk, stretch, or breathe slowly (in for 4, out for 6–8). Splash cold water on your face. Calm the body first and focus will return.

Proof log: Keep a running list of your real wins—panels, screenings, trusted collaborations, breakthroughs in your work. When doubt rises, flip through it. It's a reminder that you already belong.

Micro-belonging: Instead of chasing large communities, cultivate smaller connections. Share a frame, a short note, or a check-in with a smaller set of colleagues. These small ties are enough to keep your nervous system balanced.

Craft as community: Let the rhythm of your work be your companion. Daily rituals of creating—even small ones—remind you that your lantern is already carried by someone: you.

33
BELONGING WITHOUT CONDITIONS

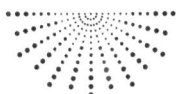

We all want to belong—to be wanted, invited, included. That hunger can blur the line between true belonging and conditional acceptance, where your ability to belong is governed by your readiness to comply with conditions, even if they violate your own boundaries. That isn't belonging; it's a transaction.

True belonging makes room for your boundaries. It doesn't collapse when you say no because it sees your presence as valuable.

Self-worth shouldn't be negotiated. It shouldn't come when others include you. It should come from knowing that your light shines regardless of whether others gather around it or not.

A lantern doesn't beg to be taken in. It burns where it stands. The right people will find its glow.

PRINCIPLE

Belonging allows boundaries. If a "no" breaks the deal, it's transactional, not belonging.

Practice

Name the offer: Open invitation or conditional? If participation requires nonnegotiable yeses for things that may cross your boundaries, call it transactional.

Check if your boundaries are respected: Give one clear no ("I'm in —but not on weekends") and watch the response—do they adjust or do they apply pressure?

State one nonnegotiable: What happens? Are you still in, or did they shut the door on you?

Use a clean "no" to provide clarity: "I'm aligned with the goal, not this tight timeline. Here's what I can deliver by Friday." Evaluate how it is received.

Exit cleanly when needed: "These requirements exceed my bandwidth. I'll hand off by [date] with notes."

Reflection

- Did I violate any boundary of mine to feel like I belong this month? Why did I do that?
- Who consistently respects my "no," and how can I build a deeper relationship with them?
- What do I fear when I say no—and what one small step can I take that would reduce that fear?

34

PEOPLE, PEACE, AND PRINCIPLES

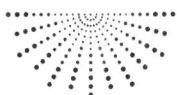

*E*very ask carries weight. Sometimes it's the weight of keeping a relationship, sometimes it's the weight of protecting your peace, and sometimes it's the weight of standing by your principles.

When these collide, clarity is everything. If you give in for the sake of a relationship with someone but lose your peace, resentment will soon follow. If you protect your peace but abandon your principles, you'll feel hollow. If you hold your principles and lose the relationship, you may feel lonely.

The lantern way is this: Choose in a way that keeps the light steady. Sometimes that means silence, sometimes a gracious close-out, sometimes walking away. But never let persistence from others decide for you.

PRINCIPLE

When asks collide, let your peace and principles outweigh other people's pressure

PRACTICE

Weigh the Three: Write: Does this protect people, peace, and principles?

Name the Cost: Note what you'd lose if you said yes.

Choose the option that keeps your light steady.

With our approach set, next we learn to name and manage the partnerships we step into.

HUSTLEWOOD AND
OPPORTUNISM

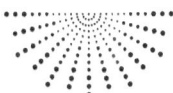

*E*very creative field has a marketplace—the rooms, threads, mixers DMs, and panels where projects first get traction. I call this Hustlewood.

Hustlewood isn't evil. It's where small doors sometimes swing open, where a short conversation becomes a first chance. It's also unstable ground. Relationships formed around timing and convenience can dissolve quickly when the benefit ends.

The problem isn't hustling; every artist hustles at some point. The problem is mislabeling it.

Bring discernment to this. Not cynicism. Don't call opportunism "betrayal." From the other person's point of view, it was always just a hustle. It ended, as hustles always do. If you see it clearly for what it is, you won't feel betrayed when it ends.

Don't mistake a flash of lightning for sunrise.

Partnerships can thrive, but they can also snap under weight. Let weight and friction reveal the truth about them, a truth that is rarely visible in calm. A truth that only reveals itself when pressure arrives— a no, a delay, a clash, a boundary. Some partnerships bend; others snap.

This section is also about the tests that reveal structure. The small frictions that are survivable, the fires that are not, and the moments when weight exposes whether a bridge can hold. It's also about welcoming early clarity, even when it hurts, because cheap clarity can save you from costly collapse later.

Resilience here is not about keeping everyone on your team. It's about recognizing who proves steady under stress, and letting the rest go.

PARTNERSHIPS

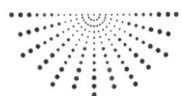

*M*ost pain comes from confusing the type of relationship you're in. Name it first; give it the energy it deserves—no more, no less.

SACRED PARTNERSHIPS

Built on trust, shared values, and mutual risk, sacred partnership ties survive pressure and time. Invest here.

HUSTLE PARTNERSHIPS

Built on timing, transaction, and convenience, hustle partnerships are useful, but are often short-lived. Scope them, time-box them, and let them end cleanly.

UTILITY PARTNERSHIPS

Utility partnerships are paid, and are bounded by an exchange of skills. Communicate a clear scope, clear rate, and clear credit. Keep it respectful. These relationships are essential but are not fellowship.

Confusing hustle for sacred—or wanting depth from a utility partnership—leads to heartbreak. If you give sacred energy to a hustle, when it dissolves (as hustles do), you will feel betrayed.

Don't offer loyalty where only convenience is expected.

RIGHT-SIZE THE RELATIONSHIP

Once you learn to identify and name the type of relationship, you can give it the right amount of your energy.

PRINCIPLE

Don't moralize the relationship. Identify it and right-size your contribution to it. Invest the most energy in your sacred partnerships. Scope and time-box the hustle. Protect the sacred partnerships by ensuring clarity, agreement, and regular communication.

PRACTICE

Label the relationship: For your own clarity, call it sacred, hustle, or utility.

Choose a container: Pick a shape that protects you: a short contract, a small milestone, a fixed number of hours.

Watch the first boundary: Say no to something small. If they adjust, continue. If they press, tighten the container or step away.

HELPFUL LANGUAGE FOR SCRIPTS AND CONTAINERS

Scope a hustle neatly: "Glad to explore. Let's keep it simple: one week, one deliverable, $X. We'll reassess after."

Time-box your energy: "I can give this two hours on Friday. If we need more, we'll schedule a follow-up."

Set a clean boundary: "Thanks for asking. That's not for me."

Decline with redirection: "I can't join a live brainstorm. If helpful, I can send three notes by Tuesday."

Close the loop when pressed: "I've given you my answer and won't be revisiting it. Wishing you the best moving forward."

RELATIONSHIP ORBITS

*G*ive every relationship the appropriate level of effort and attention.

At the lower tier, when the work overlap is minimal, the needs are different, or the investment required doesn't match the return, you don't have to cut off the relationship. You can simply shift it into the **outer orbit**: cordial, minimal, professional when needed, and with no expectation of closeness.

You might still exchange an occasional email or a quick call. This is clarity. You're signaling: *I acknowledge the relationship, but I don't confuse it for more than what it is.*

Start with these three orbits (feel free to create more for your unique situation):

INNER ORBIT (ALIGNMENT)

Your inner orbit includes people who share your vision, values, and way of working. Trust is built in, the mix creates momentum, and the relationship fuels both you and the project.

Example: a cinematographer who not only shoots beautifully but thinks in the same rhythm of story you do.

UTILITY ORBIT (SCOPED SKILL)

Your utility orbit are people you bring in for a specific, paid skill. You may not share style or long-term vision—and that's fine. The relationship is bounded—clear scope, clear rate, clear credit.

Example: a marketing expert you wouldn't vacation with, but who knows how to place your film in the right channels.

OUTER ORBIT (CORDIAL TIE)

People you keep on polite, minimal terms comprise your outer orbit. You exchange small favors when appropriate and maintain a bridge in case you cross paths again. No extra energy, no implied closeness.

The common trap is confusing these: expecting a utility hire to behave like an aligned partner or reducing an aligned partner to a pure transaction. Both create resentment.

PRINCIPLE

Keep your orbits clear:
    Inner → alignment and shared vision
    Utility → paid, scoped contribution
    Outer → cordial, minimal entanglement

PRACTICE

Spend time journaling and gaining clarity on how placing people in orbits is helping to preserve your energy and prevent mismatched expectations.

STRESS-TESTING PARTNERSHIPS

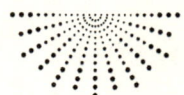

Good times hide structural issues. Pressure and challenges reveal them.

Use the following four quick tests to see what a partnership is made of—before you bet your time, energy, or name on it.

TEST: TIME AS A TELL

How someone handles shared time shows their priorities, clarity, and respect. Small windows are enough: a 30-minute call, a work session, a notes pass.

What to look for

After you meet, do you feel lighter and sharper—or drained and restless?

Do they arrive prepared, land decisions, and end on time? Or do they sprawl, waffle, and add work without moving the ball?

PRINCIPLE

How they treat time is reliable evidence of their value as a partner. Believe it.

PRACTICE

After each session, write one phrase: *lighter/sharper* or *drained/restless*.

Don't explain away patterns. Upgrade partners who multiply your hours; downgrade—or exit the partnership of—those who waste them.

Protect your best time blocks for the people who use them well.

TEST: FRICTION VS. FIRE

Every partnership and collaboration has rough edges.

People fumble, miss deadlines, miscommunicate. That's friction—frustrating, but survivable.

But not all imperfection is the same. Some patterns ignite fire—guilt-trips, conditional belonging, retaliation—when you set boundaries. Fire doesn't just slow you down; it consumes you.

DISCERNMENT TIP

Friction looks like: lateness, disorganization, clashing styles—but paired with accountability and recovery.

Fire looks like: manipulation, blame, pressure to erase your boundaries—with no willingness to own their part.

PRINCIPLE

Work with imperfect people; don't work with people who burn you.

PRACTICE

Name the issue. Did they own it and recover? → Friction: continue, but with new guardrails.

Manipulation or pressure? → Fire: stop, contain, or exit.

Log incidents. One spark can be an accident; a pattern is a forecast.

TEST: SAYING NO

Your first no is the cleanest stress test. Say it once, then watch.

A true partner respects your boundaries, shares your values, and carries risk with you.

A problematic partner flatters when they need you, presses hard when you say no, and downplays the danger they are asking you to bear. If you step back, they label it betrayal.

The test is simple: what happens after your first no?

If the relationship remains steady, you've found a true, valuable partner.

If the relationship fractures, you've dodged a bullet. Consider yourself lucky and move on.

Early clarity saves you from deeper wounds. It hurts in the moment, but it's protection in the long run.

Not every lost partnership is a missed opportunity. Sometimes it's a bullet you didn't take.

PRINCIPLE

A partnership that can't absorb one no won't carry weight later.

PRACTICE

Use one clean no: Say it once, kindly, without overexplaining.

Observe, don't argue: Note their response over 7–14 days (is it pressure or do they respect your decision?).

Decide and document: If the partnership fractures, close the loop and journal what you learned.

TEST: CHEAP CLARITY

When someone reveals their true nature early—by snapping at a no, cutting ties suddenly, closing the door on you—it hurts. But it's also a gift. I call it cheap clarity.

Imagine discovering that same flaw after years of shared work, signed contracts, or public commitments. The cost would be devastating.

Early clarity may feel like pain, but it's protection. Better to lose a brittle partner now than to lose your peace later.

Every subtraction sharpens your direction.

PRINCIPLE

Treat a closed door like hard-won data. It's clarity that'd otherwise cost you time, effort, money and opportunities to obtain.

PRACTICE

Name the learning: One sentence—*What did this closure clarify?*

Reallocate energy: Move the freed time to one sacred partner or your own project today.

Retire the thread: Archive the emails/DMs so your mind stops revisiting them.

Reset your filters: Add what you learned to your next intake (time, scope, credit, decisions).

Summary:

Time tells you the truth.

Friction is human; fire is harm.

One no is the bridge test.

Early clarity is a gift—bank it and move on.

Let pressure do the sorting so your lantern's fuel goes where it burns bright.

39
OPPORTUNISM

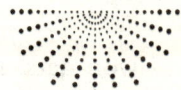

*I*n creative industries, many relationships start with timing and convenience. That's normal hustle.

Opportunism is different: you get praise when you're useful, pressure when you set a boundary, and silence when you're no longer needed.

Don't moralize it—recognize it early so you right-size your energy and save your best fuel for partners who stand with you long after the optics fade.

PRINCIPLE

Don't moralize the relationship; identify opportunism early and right-size your investment.

PRACTICE

Run these three tests:

The Face Test

Here are some ways you can recognize opportunists.

They use flattery as leverage.

They hand out big compliments, then jump straight to asks that cross your boundaries.

Example: "You're exactly who we need. Could you add your name on our deck ASAP?"

Their pressure tactics are dressed up in the language of friendship or kindness.

You say no once. But they keep circling back with guilt or urgency.

Example: You clearly refuse to do a free consult. But they still send three follow-ups: "It's just this once."

They are soft with powerful people, and hard with you.

They are deferential with a famous producer, but make unreasonable demands of you.

Example: They'll wait weeks for a big name but want your overnight turnaround.

They give gifts with strings attached, tracking it in their "ledger."

These favors later come due for collection, far outside context.

Example: "Remember when I introduced you to X? Now you owe me this contract."

The Math Test

Opportunists rank people by visibility and convenience. When the "math" changes, their behavior towards you changes as well.

Tells to watch: lots of warmth when you or your project is popular, cold when not. They are more excited about your wins and industry contacts than they are with the excellent quality of your work. A quick question to ask yourself: Are they here for what I make, or for who I'm next to?

The Reciprocity Test

Strip away your badges in your mind. No awards, no titles, no possibility of making introductions. Now ask: How would they treat you? Would they respect your first no? Would they give you credit and pay you for your work? If yes, you have reciprocity. If not, you're in a power play.

40

RESILIENCE OF RELATIONSHIPS

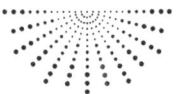

*R*esilience is not only personal. It also lives in the space between people as well as in the relationship itself. A bond is not *you* or *them*, but a third lantern, co-created and co-tended.

But not all bonds carry resilience in the same way.

Family ties often bend without breaking. History, love, and shared roots give them elasticity. A red flag here may not mean the end; it may be a call to pause, renegotiate, or heal. A resilient family bond is one that survives imperfection because the shared story is stronger than the fracture.

Professional ties, by contrast, are built on trust, respect, and reciprocity. Their resilience is measured in clarity, not elasticity. When those foundations crack, repair is rare. A red flag here is not a pause but often a signal to step back, release, or protect your flame.

In both cases, resilience is not carried by one person's willpower. It asks for co-stewardship. You can bring grace, patience, or forgiveness, but unless the other person also tends the lantern, it will sputter.

PRINCIPLE

Relationships are third lanterns. Their resilience depends on two people choosing to light and relight them together.

PRACTICE

Name the lantern: See the bond as its own entity, not just your responsibility.

Read the red flags wisely: In family, they may call for repair. In professional ties, they often call for release.

Test the co-stewardship: Are both of you tending the flame? If not, no amount of your effort alone will sustain it.

Protect the inner flame: Whether you repair or release, your first duty is to your lantern within.

REFLECTION

Some lanterns endure because of history. Others endure because of choice. Know which you're holding—and never mistake one for the other.

SPOTTING RED/GREEN FLAGS

Red flags
- Praise is followed by scope creep
- Pushback after a clear no from you
- Vague about credit, precise about your obligations
- Their urgency always becomes your problem
- One tone in public, another in private

Green flags
- Clear scope and timelines on both sides
- Your first no is respected and accepted
- Credit is offered early, not negotiated later
- They bring something to the table before asking for more

– Same tone whether the room is powerful or not

On Worth

Opportunistic people make calculations. They don't always push boundaries evenly. With those they see as highly connected, visible, or costly to lose, they tread carefully. With those they assume have less leverage, they press harder, believing the fallout won't matter.

This is the nature of opportunism: misreading leverage as worth. It treats relationships not as mutual commitments but as risk assessments.

The truth is different. True worth isn't calculated by others. It's carried within. It shows up in your craft, your principles, your persistence, and your lantern's steady light. If someone treats you as expendable, that reveals more about their values than your value.

The lesson: Don't confuse someone else's calculation with your reality. You may not always be the person they're afraid to lose, but that doesn't mean you aren't invaluable. And when you stand by your principles, you make it clear that you can't be bought, pressured, or bartered.

Let others play their calculation game. Your work and your boundaries are your true value.

Don't Accept Favors From Opportunists

In creative communities, favors are common: a shared contact, a few hours of studio time, a workshop invite. At their best, favors are gifts —freely given, no strings attached. Sometimes, though, they're disguised transactions.

I call this the ledger trap.

For example, you accept some favors from someone, who then turns around and feels entitled to ask you for something far beyond the scope of the favor they did for you. It may even exceed the limit of friendship or professional courtesy.

When you decline, they may keep pressing, and act as if your boundary doesn't exist.

Their gratitude turns into a guilt trip: "I did this for you, so you owe me." If you still refuse, they recast your no as betrayal—going cold, pulling away, or shutting you out.

At its core, this is a power play.

They are treating their favors as currency while you may treat them as gifts. You're not playing the same game.

The tell: A true gift carries no debt. A transaction disguised as a favor always comes due.

Set the principle: I don't accept favors where the expected return is undefined or asymmetric.

What asymmetric looks like: the favor they gave you cost them very little (a two-line intro, a few hours at a studio that served their needs as much as yours), but the return they demand costs you a lot (a weekend rewrite, a free consult, a legal or reputational risk to you). They call those equal. But to you, they are not.

If someone shows you their gift has strings, don't accept it. If they try to trap you in their favors debt, step out of the game.

A lantern doesn't owe its light to anyone who demands it. It shines freely, or not at all.

RELIABILITY

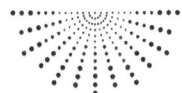

One of the hardest things to know is who is truly reliable—who's in your corner for real, and who's only around when it's convenient. You usually only find out in moments of stress or conflict, when masks slip.

That's where clarity comes. Some people will remove themselves when they realize your no is firm. That's cheap clarity. Others will go further. They may spin, complain, or speak against you. And here's the hidden gift: if their words cause someone else to pull away from you, that person was never fully with you either.

This is the add-on benefit: Their spin does the pruning for you. Instead of wasting months nurturing fragile relationships, they self-select out.

What remains is a circle of people who know you by your work and by your steadiness, not by gossip. Your task isn't to chase or defend. It's to note who stays steady through storms.

That's your inner circle. Everyone else is noise.

42

READ THE AMBERS

*L*ife gives you signals like traffic lights. Some are red—clear stops. Some are green—obvious go-signals. But most are amber—uncertain, in-between.

The amber light is where discernment lives. Do you slow down, or do you speed up and try to make it through the intersection?

Not every hesitation means no. Not every opening means yes. Wisdom lies in reading the ambers, pacing yourself with the signals life gives, and knowing which ones to honor.

PRINCIPLE

Discernment is resilience in real time.

PRACTICE

Spot the amber: Write down one decision you're sitting on. Is it truly red (stop), green (go), or amber (uncertain)?

Pause before action: With ambers, delay commitment by 24 hours before deciding.

Name the signal: After the delay, label it clearly: red, green, or green light disguised as amber.

CURRENCY OF INTEGRITY

*I*n a hustle economy, people trade favors, names, quick wins. But integrity is a slower currency. It doesn't buy applause today, but it builds reputation that lasts for years.

When you refuse an ask you can't stand behind, you may lose a relationship—but you keep the asset that compounds: your credibility.

A lantern that burns clean may not flare as bright in the moment, but its light will last through the night.

PRINCIPLE

Hold your line even if it costs you a momentary win.

PRACTICE

Say no to what you can't sign your name to.

Credit exactly what you did; don't inflate, don't erase.

Keep the promises you make; don't make ones you can't keep.

Write one "line I won't cross" and keep it visible.

BE THE STEADY LIGHT

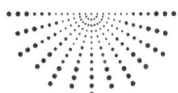

*I*t's easy to spend time judging who stayed, who left, who spun. But the harder, deeper question is this: What kind of collaborator am I?

While others falter, you can choose to be the one who doesn't. The one who doesn't spin when things sour. The one who honors boundaries instead of pressing past them. The one who shows up steadily, again and again, with no agenda beyond care, respect, and the work itself.

Reliability isn't only something you demand from others. It's something you practice so others can rely on you without fear. It's choosing to stand in someone else's light with gratitude, not grasping. It's being a partner whose presence steadies the room instead of clouding it.

The world has enough noise, enough betrayal, enough hustle-for-self.

A lantern is different. A lantern steadies not only its own light but offers that steadiness for others too.

Be the reliable one.

Be the gracious one.

Be the light you once wished was standing beside you.

PRINCIPLE

Set your standard before you judge others'.

PRACTICE

Write a one-line collaborator standard. My one line standard for every collaborator I work with is that they care about the story/project and understand it at a deep level. If it's just a gig for them, that's totally fine, but then they are transients in my artistic life)

Do one reliability act every project (show up early, send the 24-hour follow-up, meet the exact spec).

When tempted to vent, send a steady, factual note instead.

45

INTERLUDE: THREADS
OF RESILIENCE

*E*very creative journey has a hidden chapter no one likes to write about: The moment you stop wanting to continue pursuing the dream.

Sometimes you just break. A project stalls. A deal falls apart. Recognition doesn't come. And the effort you've poured into it for years feels wasted. In that moment, you don't want to bounce back. You don't want to finish the script, or submit the cut, or even open the project file again.

This is the mountain nobody talks about—not rejection, not criticism, but indifference. The moment when the work feels pointless, and the dream feels like it belongs to someone else.

Here, resilience doesn't begin with energy or drive. It begins with the smallest threads:

A flicker of curiosity—*What if this idea still has life in it?*

A scrap of hope—*What if the next draft works better?*

A brief desire—*I want to see this scene finished, just for me.*

A moment of generosity—*I promised someone a version, and I want to keep my word.*

A flash of grace—*I'll give this project one more day, even if I don't believe in it fully at this time.*

Those threads are enough. You don't need to feel inspired. You don't need to feel certain. You only need to hold one thread until another shows up. That's what keeps the lantern lit through the midnights of the work.

Resilience isn't about charging ahead with fire—it's about refusing to drop the thread when everything in you wants to walk away.

46

COMMUNITIES

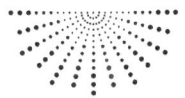

*C*ommunities can lift us, but they can also whisper against us. We must see systems for what they are and discern open doors from closed clubs.

Once you know your own footing, you can step into circles with clearer eyes. Communities are not judges handing down verdicts on your worth—they are systems, each with their own operating rules. Some are open, some are closed, some are generous, some are political.

This section is about seeing communities without illusion. About recognizing that some will serve you, some will use you, and some will never open their gates no matter how much you give. Clarity here frees you from chasing what cannot be caught.

A lantern doesn't beg at the gate. It shines where it stands, and the right circles form around it.

SYSTEMS, NOT JUDGES

*I*t's easy to imagine community as an external force—a crowd watching, evaluating, deciding who's in and who's out. But in truth, most communities are just systems. Groups of people working together for a purpose, each with their own constraints, costs, and benefits.

Once you see it that way, the fear of rejection softens. A community isn't aiming its judgment at you; it's simply running its own operating system. And you get to decide: Does the exchange make sense? Do the benefits outweigh the restrictions and costs?

But some communities aren't open systems. They are exclusive clubs. In those cases, membership is not a matter of how much you're willing to give. It's either granted or it is not—often for reasons outside your control (pedigree, politics, timing, luck). The mistake is to treat these clubs as destiny, as if your worth depends on whether you get invited. It doesn't.

The lantern way is this: recognize the difference. With open systems, calibrate your engagement. Choose in or out based on value. With exclusive clubs, accept that the gate may never open. That's not failure. That's simply their system, not yours. Build your own circle.

The lantern doesn't wait for the door to open. It shines where it stands.

48

WHISPER TEST

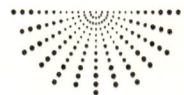

*I*n creative fields, communities are both lantern and shadow. They can amplify your light, but they can also magnify whispers. One comment, one slight, and it can feel like the whole room has turned against you.

But here's the truth: Most whispers fade. What endures isn't what's said once in frustration—it's the pattern of how you show up.

The Nature of Tight-Knit Communities:

They trade in stories. Word travels quickly, but it also loses sharpness quickly.

Perceptions are shaped less by single incidents and more by repeated behavior.

Communities respect steadiness. Someone who shows up consistently with grace will outlast someone who vents bitterness.

The Whisper Test:

When you worry someone might speak badly about you, ask:

If someone heard that about me, what would my pattern show them?

Does my behavior over time confirm or contradict the whisper?

If your pattern contradicts the whisper, you're safe. Your light will eventually outshine the noise.

Should You Join Communities?

Yes—but with perspective. Communities are not kingdoms; they're marketplaces. They can open doors, create allies, and share resources. But they cannot define your worth.

PRINCIPLE

Belonging is not guaranteed, and it should never be purchased by erasing your boundaries.

PRACTICE

Show up consistently: give, share, support where you can, without overextending.

Stay neutral in conflicts. Don't repeat whispers, don't fuel drama. Silence here is power.

Use communities as tools, not mirrors. They are places to exchange value, not measure your self-worth.

Invest in circles of depth. Two or three trusted peers matter more than dozens of loose affiliations.

REFLECTION

Communities are like stadium crowds: loud, fickle, and always moving on to the next match. Your lantern isn't meant to light the whole arena, only the path you walk and the people who walk it with you. The whisper test is simple: Keep your light steady. Let the noise pass.

49

SMALLER THAN YOU THINK

he communities that feel all-powerful are often just a few hundred people. They whisper, they judge, they posture. But the world is vast, and most real opportunities come from unexpected directions, not from the circle you fear.

If you chase reassurance from the small circle, you'll shrink yourself to fit its size. If you stand steady in your independence, you'll stay open to the bigger world—where new collaborators, new platforms, and new doors appear without warning.

Let them talk. Let them close their small doors. You don't need them anyway.

PRINCIPLE

Stand in self-reliance.

Your lantern doesn't need their oil to stay lit.

REFLECTION

Discomfort is training. Sitting in aloneness isn't punishment; it's rehearsal. This is the muscle you need for the long run, because filmmaking (and all art) is always a dance with solitude, no matter how much external noise comes with success.

50

ECHO TEST

*W*hat people say about others in front of you is an echo of what they will one day say about you. If they tear down colleagues easily, assume your name will eventually pass their lips the same way.

The instinct is to fight back, to defend yourself, to correct the record. But the stronger move is steadiness. In tight-knit circles, reputations are built less on words and more on patterns. Over time, people notice: Who keeps their grace? Who repeats the same story no matter the room? Who burns steady instead of flaring with each rumor?

Your best defense isn't counter-speech. It's consistency. A lantern doesn't echo gossip. It shines in place, long enough that the noise fades and the glow remains.

PRINCIPLE

If someone speaks badly about you, let their pattern expose itself. In the end, people trust the light they can see, not the echoes in the dark.

Reflection

Where do I hold judgments about others while disliking theirs about me?

What specific actions from them would change my view—and what actions from me would better align with my purpose regardless of theirs?

What's one step I can take this week that improves my alignment and gently improves a key relationship?

51

POLITICS OF THE ROOM

*I*n group work, whether in a conference room or a writer's room, the quality of ideas doesn't always decide what survives.

People form alliances—sometimes for reasons that have nothing to do with the craft. Fear of being overshadowed, the safety of numbers, or even simple dislike can shift the balance.

You can be right and still be voted down.

The danger is to internalize this as failure: *If they rejected me, my ideas must not have been good enough.* But often the rejection isn't about merit; it's about politics—the subtle ways people protect their own relevance, visibility, or influence.

The lantern way is to remember:

Read the room, not just the script. Notice who is aligning with whom, and why. The story on the table is only half the story.

Don't fight every battle. Sometimes letting go of a group's direction is wiser than burning your energy trying to win allies who've already chosen sides.

Keep your ideas alive elsewhere. Just because they're dropped in one room doesn't mean they're worthless. Many great projects were born from ideas abandoned by committees.

Allies and enemies will come and go. But your craft is not a vote, and your worth is not decided by alliances. A lantern shines even when the room turns its back.

Guardrail: Navigate Alliances Without Burning Out

Separate Ego From Evaluation

When alliances form against you, it's easy to feel personally targeted. Pause and ask: *Is this about my idea, or about their need to assert themselves?* Most of the time, it's the latter. Don't let their insecurity become your shame.

Bank Your Ideas Elsewhere:

Just because a group discards your contribution doesn't mean it's worthless. Archive it. Revisit it. Many discarded ideas later find life in solo projects or different collaborations. Your lantern doesn't dim just because a room looked away.

PRINCIPLE

Choose Your Investment Level

PRACTICE

Decide whether the project or room is worth your energy. If alliances are fixed, don't burn yourself fighting uphill. Contribute with grace, but quietly redirect your best energy into spaces where your voice carries weight.

Guardrail reminder: Don't confuse rejection with invalidation. Rejection in a room is often politics; validation of your craft comes from persistence, clarity, and the work itself.

REFLECTION

Be brutally honest with yourself. Sometimes an idea is rejected because the idea just isn't good for that moment, for that situation, for that story, or it just isn't good.

Don't take it personally. Keep contributing. You remain valid.

52

BOUNDARIES

    riendships can fuel us, but they can also end when boundaries arrive.

Every circle has limits. Every friendship has lines. And every artist, sooner or later, must choose: protect peace, or surrender it.

This section is about what happens when boundaries are tested, when saying no ends a tie, when silence or closure is the only way forward. It's about surviving the imbalance of fallout—when they move on lightly while you carry the heavier weight—and about transmuting that weight into clarity, craft, and gold.

Breakups don't end your light. They refine it. A lantern that guards its flame can survive loss without losing itself.

FEAR OF CONNECTION

*W*hen relationships have ended painfully in the past, your nervous system remembers. It learns: *Connections don't last—protect yourself.* That memory isn't just thought; it's felt in the body as tension, hesitation, or guardedness. So when a new collaboration feels close, you may react with extra caution, or with the opposite—over-giving in hopes of securing safety.

Neither response is wrong. Both are just echoes of past rupture. But steadiness comes when you name the moment clearly: *This is a gift, not a guarantee.* If the connection lasts, that's grace. If it fades, the gift has still served.

A lantern doesn't demand that every flame it meets join its own. It carries its light forward, grateful for sparks that mattered in their time.

PRINCIPLE

Closeness in creative work is real, but it isn't always permanent. A collaboration can feel like deep connection in the moment, but that doesn't automatically mean friendship or forever. Treat each exchange as a gift for the season it belongs to, not a promise beyond it.

PRACTICE

Name the value: Before saying yes, ask: *What do I gain? What do they gain?* If there's growth or learning for you, it's sustainable.

Notice your body: If you feel tense, over-invested, or on guard, pause. Ask: *Is this my nervous system remembering the past, or the present reality?*

Hold it lightly: Remind yourself, *This may not extend past the project, and that's okay.*

Discern spark from bond: After the work ends, pause. Was this just a spark for the moment, or a bond worth carrying forward?

Release the rest: Let go of the "it should last" story. Some connections light the path briefly without becoming lifelong fires.

JUST SAY NO

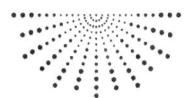

a boundary isn't a debate. It's a lantern line—once drawn, it holds

The pull tc explain is strong—to justify, soften, or bargain your way to peace. But every extra paragraph burns fuel. A clear no, offered once and with grace, is enough.

No is not hostility. No is clarity. It protects your energy for the work that matters, the people who respect you, and the principles that keep you steady.

True friendship isn't measured by favors; it's measured by whether your boundaries are honored. If a single no turns you into "not a friend," the bcnd was convenience, not care. When pressed after a clean no, you have two options: silence or a final close-out. Anything beyond that weakens the light.

A lantern doesn't brighten for every hand that reaches. It burns steady because it guards its flame.

PRINCIPLE

No is a full sentence. Real friendship respects your no.

If one boundary breaks the relationship/friendship, it was a conditional bond. Choose the response that keeps your light steady—silence or a single close-out—and let the rest go.

PRACTICE

Write your no. Keep a graceful template handy, such as "Thanks for thinking of me. I can't take this on."

Say it once. Deliver your no without autobiography or apology.

Choose your exit. If pressed, pick one: silence (finality) or a one-time close-out ("I've given my answer and won't revisit it. Wishing you the best.").

Watch the response. Respect = continue. Pressure, guilt, or re-asking = step back.

Log the pattern. If they only stay for yeses, reclassify the relationship (outer orbit—see chapter on Relationship Orbits) and redirect your energy to work aligned to your purpose.

SIGNAL EARLY

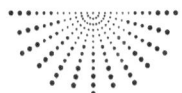

*G*race can be mistaken for availability if you don't show the edges of it. Opportunistic people often test by pushing a little further each time, looking for where you bend. If you don't signal your limits early, they may read your silence as permission.

PRINCIPLE

The key is to make boundaries visible before they're tested too far.

PRACTICE

Name your lane: When someone drifts into topics or asks outside your role, a simple "That's not my area" draws a clear line.

Use short nos: instead of overexplaining, try "That's not for me" or "I can't take that on." Brevity signals firmness.

Deflect gossip: If someone speaks badly of others, choose neutrality—"I don't engage in those conversations." One sentence can reframe the dynamic.

Match energy with clarity: If you're generous with time or

support, balance it with reminders of your priorities: "I can do this much, but not beyond."

REFLECTION

Boundaries don't weaken grace; they strengthen it. They show that your generosity has form, not just flow. A lantern doesn't light endlessly in all directions—it shines within the frame of its glass. That frame is what makes the light usable.

Signal your boundaries early, so you won't have to defend and rebuild them later.

PATTERNS

ot every red flag feels like a flag when you're in it. Sometimes it looks like common ground: Their complaint echoes your own. Sometimes it looks like momentum: a new idea, a new name, a new opportunity. Sometimes it looks like nothing at all: just one small, forgettable moment.

The truth is that patterns only reveal themselves in hindsight. A person who badmouths others will eventually badmouth you. A person who changes focus constantly will eventually scatter your trust. A person who uses pressure tactics once will use them again. The signs were there—but the promise of belonging, or partnership, or validation can be strong enough to make us overlook them.

Don't punish yourself for hope. Hope is what keeps the lantern lit. But let every overlooked sign become part of your discernment.

PRINCIPLE

Each time you see the pattern more clearly, you shorten the distance between the first red flag and the final decision.

REFLECTION

The lesson is this: You will sometimes ignore signs because you want to believe. That doesn't make you naïve. It makes you human. What matters is that once the pattern comes into focus, you act.

The lantern way is not to live in suspicion of everyone, but to sharpen your sight so that when someone shows you who they are, you don't stay in the dark.

COMMUNICATION

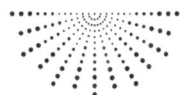

*B*oundaries decide *what* you'll engage with.

Communication decides *how*. This section gives you containers and language—first in private channels, then in public.

The fact is that your nervous system needs protection too. Often that protection comes not from *what* you do, but *how* you respond.

Sometimes the best way to clarify your own response is by speaking it aloud to a trusted friend. Their emotional distance from the event that triggered the response can help you see how best to deliver it—both in format and in content.

Talking it through can reveal insights your nervous system already feels but hasn't yet put into words.

These Lantern Learnings show you ways to handle your response, whether private or public.

PRIVATE COMMUNICATIONS

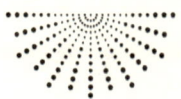

*P*rivate channels—whether one-to-one, within a team, or across teams—are meant to be just that: private.

In practice, assume anything you write could surface publicly at any time.

The 2014 cyberattack on Sony Pictures Entertainment proved it: internal emails between senior executives, including unflattering comments about stars, were exposed and widely reported.

The lesson is simple: Communicate with grace, in every channel. If your words were made public tomorrow, you should be able to stand by them.

FORMAT AS BOUNDARY

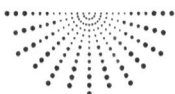

*S*ometimes the hard part isn't *what* is asked of you, but *how* it's asked.

A request over email might feel fine, but the same request as a live call can leave your nervous system buzzing. It isn't weakness. It's your body signaling that the format doesn't work for you for whatever reason.

For example, when there's a heated debate in progress, I may want to respond to a particular situation over email. Perhaps because I want to carefully weigh every word. But if I were to accept a call, my nervous system will know that I won't get the chance to defer a response until I've thought things through. The format matters.

PRINCIPLE

Resilience is not endless. The wrong format drains it faster than the wrong task. Protecting *how* you engage is as important as *whether* you engage.

PRACTICE

Name it: *It's not the request, it's the format.*

Redirect: Suggest an alternative, "I'll share my thoughts in writing."

Check your body: Notice the calm when the format fits.

Release guilt: Changing the format isn't refusing connection; it's creating the conditions to show up fully.

REFLECTION

Your nervous system is part of your discernment toolset. Listen to it. It will help you save resilience for where it matters.

REDIRECTION

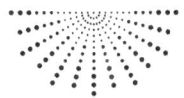

*N*ot every boundary requires the word *no*. Sometimes you protect your energy by reshaping the request instead of rejecting it.

PRINCIPLE

Boundaries land softer when you offer redirection. "No" can end the road. Redirection keeps the path intact—on terms that protect you.

Decline the terms, not the relationship.

PRACTICE

Acknowledge first: "I appreciate the ask."

Set the boundary: "A live call won't work for me right now."

Offer an alternative: "… but I can send a short note by Friday."

Close with grace: "Thanks for understanding."

GRACEFUL EMPTINESS

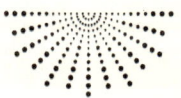

*T*here are moments when you simply have nothing to give—no bandwidth, no energy, no useful feedback. Yet the situation doesn't allow you to say no outright.

This is where brevity and gratitude become your shield. You acknowledge the ask, thank the person, and close with nothing extra. You haven't said no, but you also haven't taken on anything you can't carry.

PRINCIPLE

When you have nothing to give, acknowledgment and gratitude are enough. You don't owe more. Even emptiness can be offered with grace. A lantern that has no fuel still protects its frame.

PRACTICE

Acknowledge: "Thank you for thinking of me."
Offer warmth without substance: "I'm cheering you on."
Close cleanly: "That's all I have right now."

CLOSE THE LOOP

*W*hen pressure mounts, the temptation is to fight back, over-explain, or lash out. But that only keeps the fire burning. The wiser path is to close the loop—clearly, firmly, and with no room for debate.

A good close-out has three parts:

1. Acknowledgment—signal that you've heard the other person. ("Understood.")
2. Firm boundary—state your decision once, cleanly, without loopholes. ("I stand by my decision...").
3. Graceful exit—end with civility, not spite. ("Wishing you the best...").

This is not about winning the argument. It's about keeping your peace.

PRINCIPLE

A loop left open invites endless engagement. A loop closed with fire burns bridges. But a loop closed with clarity and grace protects your boundary, your reputation, and your lantern.

Reflection

When you close the loop, you don't just end the conversation. You teach others how to treat you—that your no is real, and that you can say it without rage or apology.

CLOSE THE LOOP
(WITH NO RESIDUE)

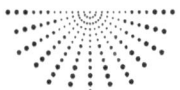

*N*ot every breakup deserves a conversation. Some only need closure.

When someone reaches out, especially after tension or distance, it's tempting to read layers into their request: *Do they want to reconnect? Do they want leverage? Do they want me to bend?*

That's the trap. The real choice isn't about their motive—it's about your bandwidth.

Closing the loop without residue means giving only what the situation requires. No more, no less. You honor your commitments, but you don't overextend. You reply with clarity, not connection; with fact, not story. The goal is to end the exchange in a single move, without leaving new threads dangling.

Sometimes that looks like a short reply. Sometimes it looks like silence. The art is in recognizing that you don't owe extra energy just because someone knocked on the door.

PRINCIPLE

Closure is clarity. Grace doesn't always mean generosity of time;

sometimes it means generosity of holding strong to a boundary, when it'd be much easier to give in and avoid conflict or discomfort.

PRACTICE

Name the ask: Is this a genuine request, or an opening for entanglement?

Meet the minimum: Offer the smallest complete response that fulfills your commitment (and nothing more).

Exit cleanly: Avoid open-ended language ("let me know how it goes"). Don't invite more than you want.

Hold the silence: If their reply is a reaction (a like, a one-word note), let it stand. Don't restart the loop.

SHARED SPACES

*L*osing one relationship in a community can feel like exile, but it's really just friction. People notice consistency more than gossip. A lantern doesn't need every circle; it needs to keep shining steadily in its chosen ones.

GUARDRAIL PLAYBOOK: NAVIGATING AWKWARD ENCOUNTERS

1. At Public Events (conventions, panels, screenings):

Keep it light: a polite nod, a "hi" if unavoidable, then move on.

Anchor yourself by talking to others—don't orbit the person you're avoiding.

If introduced in a group, stay professional: *"Nice to see you, hope you're well."* Then

pivot.

2. In Online Spaces (Discord, LinkedIn, group threads):

Don't respond to provocations or subtle digs. Silence signals steadiness.

When necessary, reply with neutral, minimal language that doesn't invite debate.

Share your work and ideas without reference to them. Build your lane.

3. Through Mutual Connections:

If their name comes up, keep your tone neutral: *"We had different approaches; I've*

moved on."

Avoid gossip—don't bad-mouth back. It positions you as the one with

composure.

Focus on your projects, not the fallout. Mutual colleagues will form their own

impressions.

4. If Confronted Directly:

Repeat your boundary calmly: *"I didn't feel qualified for that role, so I stepped back.*

That's all."

Don't elaborate. The shorter your response, the harder it is to twist.

Exit the interaction gracefully if it becomes heated: *"Anyway, I've got to head to*

[X]. Good luck with everything."

5. Internal Compass:

There's no need to turn awkwardness into hostility. Just keep your distance

instead. A perfectly fine thing to do.

Your self-worth doesn't shrink because one person cuts you off.

You are working on building your own creative world. No one gate controls

all your paths.

PRINCIPLE

Awkwardness is survivable. Civility is enough. You don't need to repair, and you don't need to retaliate. Just keep your lantern steady and, over time, the noise of one relationship fades into the background hum of the industry.

REFLECTION

The common thread in all of these is clarity. Boundaries don't always need to be loud to be real. Whether you change the format, redirect the request, or offer only gratitude, you are still protecting your light.

65

PUBLIC COMMUNICATIONS

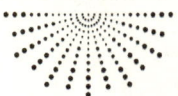

*Y*our public voice is another stage. You can flood it with noise, or you can treat it with the same craft you give your work. Silence is not absence. It is stewardship. And when you do speak, precision becomes mercy—for your audience, your circle, and your future self.

Your work speaks first. A finished scene, a short film, a frame that lingers—these are the truest parts of your public voice. But sometimes the moment asks for more—a post, a statement, a stand.

The danger is that today's world rewards volume, not depth. Quick takes win attention, but they rarely build trust. Every word you put into the world travels farther than you imagine, and impacts collaborators, communities, even family members who never chose to be part of the spotlight.

This part is about choosing your thresholds wisely—when to speak, how to stand, and how to protect your people while you do.

66

SILENCE

*S*ilence is not apathy; it's stewardship. In a culture that rewards instant takes, the rare, deliberate statement carries more weight. Speak your truth, your values, and your usefulness converge. Your audience will learn that when you light the room, it's for a reason.

PRINCIPLE

Save your voice for the moments you are best positioned and aligned with to serve. The rest could be best served by your silence.

PRACTICE

Run the 5 checks:

1. Is it True?
2. Is it Aligned with my values?
3. Is it my Filmmaker (Artist) voice?
4. Does it help someone specific?

5. Do I accept the risk of the fallout that may land not just on me, but also on my loved ones?

If the answer to any of these is no → don't post; put that energy into the work.

If *all* are yes → proceed to polishing.

POLISH YOUR POST

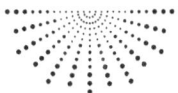

*H*eat makes sloppy writers of us all. Wait 24 hours. If your words still feel hot the next day, they're worth saying—more cleanly. Precision is mercy—to your audience, to your collaborators, to the future you who will stand beside these words later.

PRINCIPLE

If it can wait 24 hours, it should.

PRACTICE

Draft → wait 24 hours → fact-check → cut the length by 50%.

Swap one hot sentence for one source.

Ask a trusted peer for a quick red-flag read (for accuracy and unintended harm). Publish or delete.

PRECISION FOR PROTECTION

A clear message fits on a small card. Say what you believe, name what you know, admit what's uncertain, and offer one useful next step. Guard your people and your projects—do not use personally identifying information (PII) or other details that can be used to dox someone, do not make heat-of-the-moment call-outs. Conflict belongs in private channels; principles belong in public.

PRINCIPLE

Be short, sourced, and safe.

PRACTICE

Use the 4-line template:

1. What I believe—one sentence.
2. What I know—one verifiable fact + source.
3. What I don't know—name the uncertainty.
4. What I ask—one concrete action (donate/read/show up).

Set the boundary upfront: "I won't debate ad hominem or bad-faith replies."

Protect the circle: move conflict off-feed; think through impact on family/teams/ongoing work.

AVOID TAKES

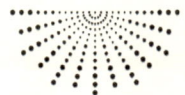

*M*ost days, let the work do the talking. Share finished or finishable things—scenes, frames, essays, how-tos. Make your feed a service lane—something people can use, learn from, or be moved by, even when you're saying nothing about the news cycle.

PRINCIPLE

Let the work be your public voice most days.

PRACTICE

Post clips/frames/micro-shorts or how-tos that help younger artists.

Share resources without commentary when that serves better than a hot take.

Host small, safe spaces (Q&A, watch party) instead of opinion threads.

ENGAGEMENT LIMITS

*O*nce you speak, don't let the comment section rent space in your mind. Decide your boundaries before you post and keep them. If you misstep, correct simply and return to your work.

The lantern isn't powered by argument; it's powered by you creating.

PRINCIPLE

You don't owe engagement.

PRACTICE

Pre-decide rules: mute/block bad-faith; reply once if a correction is needed, then move on.

If you miss: Post a brief correction, link the source, don't allow self-flagellation.

Time-box the postmortem (10–15 min), log lessons, and get back to creating.

WEIGHT OF A WORD

ords, like films, outlive their moment. A careless one can burn a bridge; a crafted one can light the way for someone else.

Resilience in public voice is not about always having the answer, or always weighing in. It's about discernment. About knowing when silence preserves your flame, and when speech extends it.

The world will keep shouting. Your strength is not in keeping pace with the noise, but in holding your ground with clarity. When you do speak, let it be a lantern: brief, bright, steady. Enough for the next step, for you and for those walking with you.

72

BREAKUPS & AFTERCARE

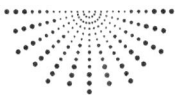

*N*ot every relationship survives the weight of boundaries. Sometimes saying no ends the relationship. When that happens, it hurts, but it reveals the truth: A bond that depends on compliance was never solid.

73
WHEN FRIENDSHIP ENDS...

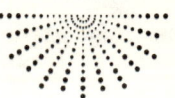

One time, when someone wanted me to do something I wasn't comfortable with, my graceful no led to pressure tactics. A firm no led to the end of the friendship.

And yet, closing out the loop was rooted in standing for my principles—self-protection, civility, professionalism, and grace. No lashing out. No recriminations. No trades of blame.

That hasn't always been my path. In the past, when a collaborator criticized my performance, I turned the spotlight back on them—insisting it was their performance that was the problem. That reflex to defend myself instead of stepping away gracefully only deepened the conflict.

Now, I've learned that the power is in restraint. When pressure escalates, the lantern way is to say no once, firmly, and then hold steady. Civility without compliance. Grace without self-harm. Professionalism without false engagement.

It can feel awkward, even costly—especially when the other person controls doors you might have hoped to walk through. But the truth is simple: Any door that demands you erase your boundaries to pass through isn't a door worth crossing.

REFLECTION

Friendship may end, but professionalism—and your lantern's steady light—can remain. Journal what you need to do to heal within yourself and to remain professional with someone who ended their friendship with you.

REACTION OVER PREPARATION

*W*hen you drive, it's wise to anticipate other people's mistakes—it keeps you safe. But in creative life and relationships, trying to predict every possible misstep from others only drains energy.

People will disappoint, misunderstand, take you for granted, or walk away. Sometimes they won't even realize they're doing it. That's not for you to prepare yourself to handle.

Your preparation is internal; your reaction standard.

Graceful.

Professional.

Boundaried.

Always. If someone cuts off a relationship, they've saved you time. If they take you for granted, they learn they can't. If they stumble, it's theirs to carry. What is yours to handle is how you respond.

Principle

Preparation in anticipation of every eventuality is exhausting. In creative life, the only preparation worth making is steadying your response.

PRACTICE

Set Your Standard – Write down in one line how you want to respond to slights, rejections, or ruptures (e.g., "professional, not personal" or "grace before closure").

Pause Before Reply – Give yourself 5 minutes before answering. Let your standard, not your impulse, speak.

Detach Outcome – Remember: Your response is the win. Whether they circle back or not is irrelevant.

FALLOUT ASYMMETRY

*I*n conflicts or ruptures, the aftermath rarely feels balanced. The other person seems to move on quickly, continuing their work, their network, their life—while you're left replaying words, drafting responses, losing sleep, carrying the emotional load.

That imbalance can feel unbearable, as if you failed because you're the one still bothered. But this is not failure. It is the price of integrity. The only way to avoid the weight would have been to cave, to abandon your boundaries, to say yes when no was true. That would have spared their feelings but hollowed your own.

The fallout is asymmetric, yes. But it is also asymmetric in opportunity. Most people burn the bridge and move on unchanged. You, however, can take the ashes and forge something new: a principle, a piece of work, a deeper clarity. That is how you turn the imbalance into gold.

PRINCIPLE

You may feel the weight long after they've moved on—but that weight is fuel.

PRACTICE

Time-Box the Fallout—Give yourself a daily window (15–20 minutes) to process the anger or hurt. Outside that window, defer the thoughts.

Anchor One Action—Each day, do one tangible task toward your creative work. Let progress re-balance the scale.

Extract the Gold—Write down one principle or insight that came from the experience. Even if no one else sees it, it becomes fuel.

REFLECTION

The asymmetry is real: You will carry more than they do. But the weight you carry can be transformed into wisdom, while theirs will simply fade into forgetfulness. That is your advantage.

76

TRANSACTIONAL RELATIONSHIPS

$\mathcal{N}$ ot all endings arrive with conflict. Sometimes they arrive quietly, when someone you've invested in chooses to move in a different direction. These are not betrayals in the dramatic sense, but they can cut just as deep—because they reveal a mismatch between what you offered and what the other person was seeking.

This is where boundaries and resilience intersect. You cannot control what someone values, but you can control how you respond when their choices leave you behind. You can let the sting harden into bitterness, or you can let it clarify your own response, which is to invest your time and energy only where respect and reciprocity live.

That's the heart of this Lantern Learning.

PRINCIPLE

Every creative path includes relationships that shift. Sometimes, despite the time, effort, or generosity you've offered, the other person chooses a different direction. The sting comes from the mismatch: You valued the relationship for its depth, while they valued it for what it could give them. Their decision may feel personal, but it's really about their priorities, not your worth.

PRACTICE

Name the Sting. Write down what hurts most: "I gave so much, and it wasn't valued." Seeing it clearly helps you separate fact from story.

Reframe the Choice. Remind yourself: *They chose what mattered most to them. I get to choose what matters most to me.* Different priorities don't diminish your own.

Reallocate the Energy. Take the energy you once gave to that connection and redirect it toward work or relationships that replenish you.

Set Your Standard. Use the experience as a boundary marker. You now know you want to build connections rooted in mutual respect and alignment, not transaction.

REFLECTION

Not everyone will walk beside your lantern. Some will turn toward other lights, even after you've shared your own. Let them go. What matters is not who stays, but how steadily you carry your flame forward once they leave.

77

MENTAL BANDWIDTH

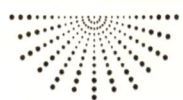

*L*etting go of a relationship in the outer world is only half the work.

The harder half happens inside—the late-night reruns, the comparisons, the "why did this happen?" loops. Even after you've released the relationship, the echoes try to live rent-free in your head.

This is where resilience needs more than boundaries. It needs bandwidth.

You can't stop every hurt from landing, but you can stop it from squatting in the space meant for your craft and your peace.

Clear your mind and let it fuel what you build with your hands.

PRINCIPLE

Bitterness, comparison, replayed slights—they all consume creative space. The trap isn't just what happened; it's how long you carry it.

When you let someone live rent-free in your mind, they steal energy you could be giving to your work, your family, your community, or your own calm.

We touched on Shah Rukh Khan's radical focus in Presence. Borrow that here: outside of gratitude, refuse to think about others.

Give your attention to what you can actually shape in this moment.

PRACTICE

Name the Tenant. When your mind circles around someone, write their name down on paper. That's the rent-free tenant. Say out loud: "I am no longer giving them space."

Swap the Space. Choose one focus that actually pays you back—working on a piece of your craft, time with a loved one, a moment of gratitude. Replace the mental loop with this concrete thought or action.

Set a Gratitude Boundary. If your mind drifts back, turn the thought into thanks: "Thank you for showing me what I don't want to invest in." Gratitude seals the door.

Anchor to Craft. Bring your attention to the smallest next thing you can do well: one shot, one phrase, one frame. For example, set a 2-minute timer and do one micro-task on your project every time the loop starts.

REFLECTION

Mental bandwidth is finite. Protect it fiercely. Evict the unpaid tenants and fill the studio of your mind with people, practices, and work that light your lantern.

UNFINISHED APOLOGIES

ot every apology repairs what was broken.

Sometimes people apologize for a detail they can live with, while leaving the deeper rupture untouched. That doesn't mean you have to pretend it's all fine.

When someone circles back with a partial apology, your nervous system may flare. Old patterns of abandonment, family rupture, or friendships lost can make you hyper-attuned to whether this is *enough*. That reaction isn't weakness—it's your body remembering old pain.

Therapy can help untangle these threads. It doesn't erase the sting of an unfinished apology, but it can show you why certain interactions feel bigger than the moment itself. It can teach you to notice the flare, ground yourself, and respond from clarity instead of reactivity.

The truth is that you don't need their apology to be whole. Your boundary, once clearly drawn, is already enough. Your lantern stays lit by your truth, not by their words, or the lack thereof.

PRINCIPLE

An apology you are given may not match the weight of what happened, but that's theirs to carry, not yours.

PRACTICE

Pause before responding. Give your nervous system time to cool.

Acknowledge without reopening. If you must reply, keep it neutral —a nod, a short "thanks," or silence.

Check your body. Notice where tension sits—breath, chest, gut. Write it down or name it out loud.

Release the ledger. Their unfinished apology is theirs to carry. You don't need to balance it.

Therapy as practice. Use the space of therapy (or journaling if you're on your own) to trace what past wounds the flare connects to. Patterns often soften once they're named.

TEND TO YOUR WOUND

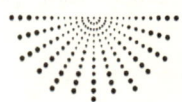

*R*esilience isn't just about standing firm in the present. It's also about facing what the present stirs from the past.

When an unfinished apology, a rejection, or a rupture hits harder than it should, it's usually because it brushes against an older wound.

That wound isn't your fault—but tending it is your responsibility. If you don't, the past quietly writes today's reactions. Every slight feels fatal, every silence like exile.

Therapy (or any structured healing practice) isn't about fixing you. It's about giving your nervous system a chance to separate *then* from *now*. It's about learning to say "This moment hurts, but it's not the whole story. I've been here before, but I'm not there anymore."

Taking responsibility for your wounds doesn't mean excusing others. It means refusing to let old injuries run your present choices. It's the difference between reacting from scar tissue and responding from clarity.

PRINCIPLE

Your wounds are not your fault, but their care is your responsibility.

PRACTICE

- Name the trigger. When your reaction feels outsized, write: "This reminds me of ___." Connect it to history.
- Find a resource or practice. Therapy, a support group, or a trusted practice space lets you unpack patterns without burdening your current work or relationships.
- Separate then from now. Say to yourself: "This is today. I survived then, and I can choose differently now."
- Choose response over replay. Pause before acting. Ask: Am I responding to this moment, or to an old wound it reminds me of?

A damaged lantern can still shine steady when the flame is tended to with care.

80
RE-CENTERING COMMUNITY

*A*fter the rupture, after the noise, after the exile—what remains? The community that never leaves—your audience, your craft, your true pack.

This section is about returning to what endures. About seeing outsiderhood as freedom, independence as strength, and interdependence as survival. It's about carrying your lantern with enough steadiness that it attracts the right pack along the way—even if it looks smaller, scrappier, or lonelier than the circles you once craved.

The lantern way is to stop chasing borrowed belonging and to build bonds that protect your peace. In the end, you don't need every circle—you just need the right ones, and you already carry their beginnings inside you.

81

AUDIENCE AS COMMUNITY

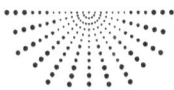

ellowships, guilds, professional groups—they matter, but they are not your truest circle. They are peers, not purpose.

Your real community is always your audience. They don't care about whispers or politics. They care only about the story you deliver: Did it move them? Did it matter? Did it stay?

A lantern doesn't exist to impress the other lanterns in the circle. It exists to guide the ones walking the path.

PRINCIPLE

When peer politics weigh heavy, return to your audience. They are the ones your lantern is meant to light.

PRACTICE

When self-doubt rises, and you feel the pressure of catering to your peer community, spend fifteen minutes writing down all the reasons you can think of why you want to serve them instead of your audience.

Then, spend another fifteen minutes writing down all the reasons why your audience needs you more than your peer community.

82

ILLUSION OF ACCELERATION

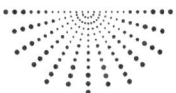

*E*very program promises acceleration. Every cohort hints that being in the right room will move you faster. And sometimes, conditions do help—peers push you, teachers challenge you, structure keeps you accountable. But no program, no teacher, no cohort can make your film for you.

I had to learn this the hard way. Watching peers complete shorts and even features, I found myself slipping into despair: *They're accelerating, I'm not.* It felt like time lost, like broken promises, like the gap between what I hoped a program would give me and what it actually could.

The truth is simpler, and harsher: Conditions aren't enough. At best, they prepare the ground. But planting, tending, and harvesting are all mine to do. My second feature won't come from waiting for acceleration—it will come from choosing, over and over, to accelerate myself.

PRINCIPLE

Comparison leads to despair. Expectation leads to resentment.

Reflection

Your only true leverage is focus. Step out of the illusion that someone else can speed you up. Step into the practice of making. The pace may not match anyone else's, but it will finally be yours.

83

OUTSIDERHOOD AS ASSET

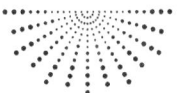

Outsiderhood isn't a handicap. It's an advantage. Instead of fighting endlessly for a seat at a shrinking table, claim the freedom of building your own. Outsiders aren't bound by gatekeepers. They create their own projects, their own intellectual property (IP), and gather their own audiences.

The upside: you control the pace, the release, and the narrative. Outsiders often define the next expansion when the contraction ends. The downside slower recognition from the "old" industry. You may never be "employed" in their sense of the word. But movements rarely start inside. They erupt from the margins—Sundance in the 1980s, YouTube in the 2000s, TikTok in 2020. None of these came from insiders protecting their seats. They came from people who had no choice but to invent their own path.

So yes, relationships matter—but maybe not *their* relationships. The ones that matter for you are with other outsiders, with audiences who respond directly, with tools and platforms that expand instead of contract. Stop grading yourself against access to the shrinking table. Start building your own table—even if it's smaller, scrappier, and lonelier.

Outsiderhood may feel lonely, but it offers freedom. Movements often start in the margins.

Framework: Outsiderhood as Brand

Name It, Don't Hide It

Acknowledge it openly: "I've always been outside Hollywood—and that's exactly why I can tell stories differently." Robert Rodriguez did it. You do it your own way.

Reframe It as Independence

Position outsiderhood as choice, not rejection: Independence lets me test ideas faster, pivot freely, and avoid compromise.

Tie It to Audience

Show that your direct link to viewers is your legitimacy: "My work speaks to audiences first, not executives."

Project Forward

Outsiderhood is temporary. When the next expansion comes, those who built in the margins will be the ones invited in—but this time it will be on their terms.

Outsiderhood is not exile. It's incubation.

The lantern shines brightest at the edges, where new movements begin.

PRINCIPLE

Exile can be incubation.

PRACTICE

Name It—Acknowledge your outsider status openly.

Reframe It—Position it as independence, not rejection.

Build your own table—Don't wait for someone to give you a seat at the table. Instead, create one project or space that doesn't need industry approval so you are not waiting, but are creating.

84
INDEPENDENCE AND THE PACK

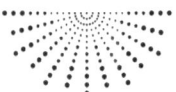

*T*he lone wolf dies. The pack survives. Right?

Independence is strength. It keeps you from shrinking yourself to fit someone else's circle, from begging at doors that don't serve you. But interdependence is survival—no career, no art, no life thrives without others.

The lantern way is to carry both. Stand steady in independence so you don't mistake noise for belonging. But stay open to the pack—to the communities, collaborators, and friends who show up in alignment, not coercion.

The test is this: Does the relationship cost your peace or protect it? If it costs, step back into independence. If it protects, lean into interdependence.

Independence without community hardens into arrogance. Community without independence collapses into dependency. Balance the two, and your lantern burns steady—bright enough for yourself, and warm enough for others.

85

THE PACK YOU CARRY

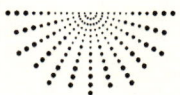

*C*ommunity doesn't have to look like everyone else's version of it. For some, it's constant gatherings and shared rituals. For others, it's a handful of steady collaborators and a body of work that draws people in.

The lone wolf doesn't die if the wolf is carrying a lantern bright enough to attract a pack along the way. Your pack may not be the old communities or the noisy circles. It may be the collaborators who show up project by project, drawn not to your small talk but to your craft.

The balance is this: craft first, a few trusted people second, noise never. If you tend your work and your inner circle you won't walk alone, even if you're never the insider at the party.

PRACTICE

Craft as magnet: Schedule time to make your work visible (snippets, frames, clips). Let your craft be the conversation starter, so you don't need to "network" in the traditional sense.

Minimum-viable pack: Choose 3–5 people who have proven

steady—collaborators, supporters, peers. Check in with them periodically, not out of obligation, but to keep the ties alive.

Low-effort presence: Don't try to join every community. Pick one or two where you can show up in your authentic role (filmmaker, educator) without having to play a persona.

Outsiderhood as angle: Frame your independence as strength. When you introduce yourself or your work, lean into the fact you're not an insider: "I've always built outside the usual circles—that's why my work looks different."

Emergency net: If survival ever becomes urgent, lean on your pack first—not on the broad, noisy communities. Build trust with a few, so you know where to turn in rough times.

86

AFTERMATH OF ACTION

*D*oing the right thing doesn't always feel good right away. Sometimes clarity brings restlessness—because part of you still craves reassurance, belonging, and proof you haven't lost the tribe. That doesn't mean the decision was wrong. It means you're human.

The lantern practice is to hold steady in the discomfort. Let time prove what your gut already knows. Peace will come later, after the agitation burns off. Restlessness is not failure—it's just the nervous system catching up to the soul.

PRACTICE

Name the Restlessness: Say it out loud or write. For example, "I feel agitated because I want reassurance." Naming it reduces its hold.

Anchor in the Body: Walk, breathe, or stretch. Remind your nervous system you're safe even without group approval.

Create Self-Reassurance Rituals: Write down three ways this decision protects your future. Read it back when doubt rises.

Limit Comparisons: Notice when you're comparing yourself to

others' partnerships or communities. Remind yourself that their path isn't your measure.

Mark Your Progress: Keep a small log of steps you've taken toward your core goals. Progress is its own reassurance.

BE THE FIRST, ANYWAY

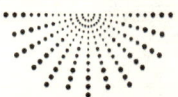

The hunger for belonging is ancient. When it isn't met, it can hijack your focus, pull you off your work, and—worst of all —rob your family of the best version of you. The people you love shouldn't get your leftovers because you're rattled by exclusion.

Yes, community can amplify success, and yes, most industries reward those who seem to belong. But every circle started with someone who didn't have one. The first filmmaker, the first actor, the first storyteller—they had no community to lean on. They lit a lantern and walked anyway.

The lantern way is this: Don't let the absence of community become an excuse or a wound that bleeds into everything else. Ground yourself in the fact that you can be the first—the one who walks without a circle and still makes the work. If belonging comes later, let it be a gift, not a requirement.

Your family, your craft, and your peace deserve the version of you that is whole, not the version of you chasing approval. The lantern doesn't wait for the crowd to gather before it shines. It shines, and the crowd gathers—or it doesn't. But the light remains.

ALONE ≠ ISOLATED

$\mathcal{W}$e often imagine resilience as the heroic rebound: the boxer up for the next round, the artist finishing the draft, the filmmaker shooting again after a collapse. But resilience isn't just one kind of move.

Sometimes it means return.

Sometimes it means redirection.

Sometimes it means release.

The measure isn't whether you come back to the same place, but whether you stay true to your flame.

Think of Prospero in *The Tempest*: After exile he regains power, then chooses to lay it down. His resilience is release, not return. Shakespeare's point stands: Discernment matters more than display.

Resilience is not armor. It's conviction.

Return: Pick up the work after the blow.

Redirect: Carry the light into a different form.

Release: Set something down to protect the deeper path.

Markers that resilience is present: you can name the hurt, you can imagine what's next, and you refuse to let bitterness write the story. The opposite isn't always collapse; sometimes it's delusion—forcing forward after the flame has gone out.

"Give me that man
That is not passion's slave..."—Hamlet

Resilience is freedom from being passion's slave—free to return, redirect, or release.

TEAM OF ONE

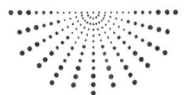

*B*efore there is a team, there is you.

When you have no crew, it can feel like you're carrying the whole weight. But no artist is truly alone. Your team is anyone whose spark fuels your work—the friend who shares a resource, the teacher whose lesson still echoes, the peer whose two-line message keeps you going. They may never sit in your credits, but their light is in your frame.

PRINCIPLE

Being a team of one isn't isolation; it's stewardship. You're responsible for the lantern, and you honor the invisible threads that help it burn.

PRACTICE

Write their names. Thank them—aloud or silently.

Remember that every scene carries more than your effort; it carries the echoes that formed you.

Stand on your own feet, and stand supported. When community wobbles, keep creating.

REFLECTION

No lantern burns in isolation.

Your light carries the light you've received from coaches, mentors, peers, and strangers, whose life lessons you've absorbed.

And you will pay it forward, whether you want to or not.

The resilience you practice will become a part of the pattern someone else will lean on.

Carry your lantern for yourself—and for the unseen eyes who notice its glow. You may never hear their thanks.

Your light will travel. That is enough.

BEYOND THE CIRCLE

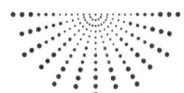

Belonging is a gift. Community is a force. Friendship is a shelter. None of these can be your flame.

Circles will shift. Some will welcome you; some will whisper behind your back; some will break up with you when you draw a boundary. You can't control that. You can control your steadiness.

Resilience in community isn't keeping everyone on your side. It's staying lit when they leave.

Your true circle is the audience who feels your work, the collaborators who hold under pressure, and the few who respect your no as much as your yes.

Every artist loses circles. The ones who last don't lose themselves.

Walk with grace. Walk with boundaries. Walk with light.

The crowd may gather or pass; the flame is yours.

Belong without bargaining.

Set boundaries without apology.

End without collapse.

Begin again, steady in your flame—carrying light that no circle can give or take away.

INTERLUDE: THE SCAR
THAT MADE MY LANTERN

There are moments that divide a life into *before* and *after*. For me, one of those moments came on the New Jersey Turnpike, tears streaming down my face, hands gripping tight on the steering wheel, heart breaking in real time.

My first feature film had finally secured distribution. It wasn't glamorous. It was a self-distribution model where I would bear the cost of the release. Yet, it was still a chance to put my work into the world. I had dreamed of this moment. I had believed in it. And then, with one phone call, it was gone.

The man on the other end held a powerful position at a large company. He withdrew the deal. No negotiation, no chance to salvage it. Just gone. I was in the middle of a Final Cut Pro editing workshop I had enrolled in as I planned for my second feature film. Instead, I abandoned the workshop to make call after call, trying to reverse this disaster.

My drive back home became a funeral procession for my dream. I cried. The tears weren't just grief for a lost opportunity, but also a recognition of how vulnerable a filmmaker truly is. How dependent I was on forces completely outside my control. How quickly the scaffolding I thought I had built just vanished.

I felt utterly alone. Powerless. At the mercy of others.

But in that pain, a seed was planted. The seed of resilience.

It didn't sprout right away. It took years. At the time, I thought I was broken. But what I eventually learned was that resilience isn't about never breaking—it's about what you do with the break. Do you stay shattered, or do you find a way to reassemble yourself, stronger at the cracked seams?

That scar—that drive, those tears, that loss—became the scar that shaped the lantern. It's the reason I'm writing this book. Because if I had to walk through that darkness, then maybe the light I found in rebuilding can guide someone else too.

Resilience isn't a glamorous word. It doesn't make you a star. It doesn't guarantee success. But it does mean that when the deal collapses, when the phone call guts you, when the tears fall in solitude, you eventually find a way to stand again. To keep going.

And in that way, scars aren't just wounds. They are lanterns. They glow faintly at first, but, over time, they illuminate the path forward.

ACT III

92
EVOLVING

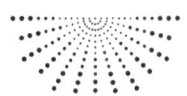

*C*arrying a lantern changes you. The longer you walk, the more storms you face, the more you discover that resilience is not endless. It must be practiced and renewed. This act is about that practice.

In *Evolving*, in addition to Grit, Productivity and Alchemy, you'll also learn practices for rest, recovery, and perspective, because resilience is not just pushing harder, it is knowing when to pause, redirect, or release.

With these principles, your lantern becomes more than a tool you carry. It becomes part of who you are. You emerge steadier, clearer, and more capable of lighting the way for others.

WISDOM IS EVERYWHERE

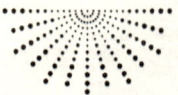

I hesitate to admit it, but you don't really need this book. If you stay open—heart and mind—the world will hand you the same lessons. However, this book provides a shortcut to that learning, a way to prepare for those life lessons, so hopefully it will not take you as long to learn them as it did for me.

I see it when I watch my son play soccer, often as a goalie. There is no better teacher of resilience than watching a group of ragtag kids become a team, learning to trust one another, even clawing their way back from behind to snatch a win.

I see it in the people who inspire me. I don't need to know them personally—I can learn from their mistakes, their patterns, their choices. I can role-play their steadiness or their courage until it becomes a part of my own way of thinking.

94

THE GAME MUST GO ON

Filmmaking is like soccer. Win or lose, the game doesn't end There's always another match.

Win, and the temptation is to celebrate forever. Lose, and the instinct is to collapse in defeat. But the truth is the same either way: Tomorrow, there's another game. Another project. Another chance to put your craft on the field.

Each film is just one match. You gather your team, step onto the field, and play your best. Sometimes you win festivals, funding, or acclaim. Sometimes you lose with silence, rejection, or failure. Both outcomes matter, because both are fuel.

A lantern doesn't burn brighter because of one night. It burns because it keeps being lit, again and again.

REFLECTION

Resilience means showing up again and again—not because every game is a victory, but because every game is part of a season.

The career of a filmmaker, like the career of an athlete, is measured not by one match but by the persistence to keep playing.

95
GO WIDE

W atching my kid play goalie, I saw a mistake that turned into a lesson. The defender passed him the ball, and instead of kicking it wide, he kicked it straight down the middle. It went straight to the opponent, who turned it into a goal. His coach told him: *Always go wide*. Even if there's no one to receive it, even if the ball goes out of bounds, the risk is smaller. A throw-in at midfield is far safer than handing your opponent a golden chance.

The creative world works the same way.

When you're under pressure, the temptation is to play the "middle" —the obvious move, the risky compromise, the thing you think will get you seen quickly. But playing it safe down the middle often feeds the opponent—bland work, generic pitches, half-fit partnerships. They take the ball and run with it, leaving you on your back foot.

Going wide looks riskier in the moment. It might mean a strange project, an unconventional path, or even letting something go "out of play." But wide clears the danger. Wide gives you time to reset. Wide keeps you from handing over your momentum to someone else.

REFLECTION

The lesson: Don't feed the middle. Go wide. Even if it looks like a loss on the surface, it protects the game you're really playing—the long one.

STUDY YOUR MODELS

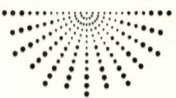

*W*hen conflict flares, instinct pulls you into defending yourself, correcting the record, or chasing belonging. But one of the steadiest compasses you can carry is this: *What would the filmmakers I admire do?*

Your models—whether M. Night, Nolan, DuVernay, Cameron, or an indie visionary who keeps creating against the odds—may share certain traits when faced with pettiness or conflict:

1. They Don't Chase the Conflict

They let the noise fade. Their attention belongs to the work, not to every whisper or slight.

2. They Preserve Grace

If they respond at all, it's brief and neutral. A single line like, *"Wishing you the best moving forward."* Nothing defensive, nothing bitter. Something that, if repeated, reflects only steadiness.

3. They Focus on the Season, Not the Match

One bad exchange doesn't define them. They return to the work, the next project, the real audience. Their career is the season.

PRINCIPLE

Reputation isn't built on single moments. It's built on years of showing up with integrity, finishing films, and carrying oneself with calm. That pattern always outlasts whispers.

PRACTICE

When you feel pulled to react, lift your eyes to your models. Ask how they would move in this moment. Then follow their steadiness, not your own impulse. A lantern burns brighter when it remembers the larger light it belongs to.

LANTERN OF RESILIENCE

$\mathcal{E}$very principle in this book has been pointing here: grace, presence, alignment, boundaries, belonging—each is a way of keeping the flame alive. But resilience is the lantern itself. Without it, every other principle is just theory.

Resilience is not a single act of bravery or a grand return after collapse. It is the broad capacity to endure hardship and adapt to change. It's what lets us bend without breaking, recover after setbacks, and keep our inner flame intact when circumstances shake us.

But resilience doesn't always look the same. It shows up in different forms, depending on what's needed:

- **Grit** is resilience as endurance. It's the perseverance to keep showing up when things are hard, slow, or unrewarding. Grit is persistence through fatigue, boredom, and setbacks —the choice to rest, recover, and still keep going.
- **Output** is resilience as iteration and production. It's the discipline of releasing work, not as a finale but as part of a rhythm. Output turns resilience into action—publishing the draft, shipping the version, showing the work even before it

feels finished. Where grit keeps you standing, output keeps you moving.

- **Alchemy** is resilience as transformation. It's the ability to take failures, wounds, and endings and turn them into fuel, meaning, and light for what comes next. Where grit keeps you in motion, alchemy changes the motion itself.

Together, Grit, Output and Alchemy form the three sides of resilience. One steadies you, one carries you forward, and one remakes you. All three matter. Resilience is the art of staying lit, even when the path disappears—and learning to move, release, and remake as the terrain shifts.

GRIT: RESILIENCE
AS ENDURANCE

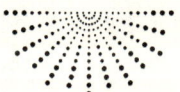

The following learnings are grouped lightly within sections for Grit, Output and Alchemy. But they do interact quite a bit. So do bear that in mind as you go through these.

Let's start by focusing on Grit. How does Grit show up?

Grit shows up as persistence and endurance—you keep going, even when progress is invisible to you.

RESILIENCE OR DELUSION

*R*esilience is not glamorous. It is not even always noble. It is survival—choosing to keep walking when the ground has collapsed. But resilience has a shadow twin: delusion. To keep going at all costs can mean ignoring reality, refusing to grow, or refusing to listen. The line between resilience and delusion is thin.

I have spent years learning how to walk that line. How to keep moving without lying to myself. How to separate rejection of a film from rejection of me. How to admit that if the craft isn't landing, it means there's more to learn. How to care for my family and my health alongside the work, so I don't mistake obsession for resilience.

That moment on the turnpike was my first collapse. But it was also my first step into resilience. Every principle in my lantern grows from that seed. The lesson is not to romanticize suffering. The lesson is that resilience must be tethered to truth.

PRINCIPLE

To be resilient is to survive the night without mistaking it for dawn. To be delusional is to call the night daylight. The lantern is what keeps you from that mistake: a steady flame, showing just enough light to take the next step—with both hope and honesty.

REFLECTION

Do you think you need to have a little bit of delusion to be in the creative industry trying to "make it" as an artist? Or do you need a lot? Is there a different thing you could go after instead, such as resilience?

TEND THE FIRE FIRST

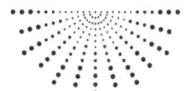

*C*reative priorities are rarely just about deadlines. They are about energy. You can't pour steady light outward if your inner fire is flickering.

Sometimes the work that demands your time is not the most urgent on paper, but the most urgent for your spirit. When you're in flow, capture it. When a shock or setback shakes you, process it. When a principle crystalizes, write it down. These moments aren't distractions from the "real" work—they are what make the real work possible.

The trap is believing you can force yourself into productivity while ignoring the turbulence inside. You may meet the deadline, but you'll bring only half of yourself to it. Tending the inner fire is what allows you to show up fully for everything else.

This doesn't mean abandoning external commitments. It means balancing the ledger: Secure your own clarity first, then turn to the assignments, the edits, the deliverables.

PRINCIPLE

By tending to your own flame, you protect the lantern's ability to shine in the world.

REFLECTION

Don't mistake flow or reflection as indulgence. They are fuel. When you tend your own fire first, you turn persistence into resilience—not just surviving the journey but sustaining your light along the way.

101

GRANTED STAGES, CHOSEN VOICES

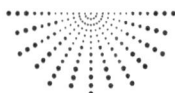

*M*any opportunities in a creative career are *granted*, not self-made. A festival accepts your film. A panel invites you to speak. A company selects you for a grant. Each feels like access —but it's borrowed light, not your own. The spotlight can shift at any moment. Others may crowd in, or it may be taken away entirely.

The truth is that you can't control the granting. What you *can* control is what you do when the light is briefly yours. If you stand in it with clarity, if your voice is distinct and your work is solid, even a moment of access leaves a lasting impression.

Your control is in continuing to build your own lanterns—the projects, platforms, and communities you can light without waiting for permission. A mailing list, a film on YouTube, a course, a book— these are commodities no one can take from you.

So when a granted opportunity arrives, accept it with gratitude but not dependence. Let it amplify your voice, not define it. And remember: If the invitation is withdrawn tomorrow, your lantern still shines.

REFLECTION

The path is long, and the spotlight is fickle. Keep your light steady.
    This way you hold two truths:
    Yes, access is often controlled by others.
    But your worth is not.

102

SOLO AND UNSEEN

*B*eing solo and unseen can feel empty, but it is also a gift. Enjoy it while it lasts. With no eyes watching, no audience judging, you are free to wrestle with your own craft. This is the purest collaboration—the one you have with yourself—your mind, your ideas, your desires—the opportunity to discover your voice before others arrive to shape it. In this time, you discover your voice, learn to challenge it, and learn to grow against it while allowing it to grow.

One day, you may be surrounded by teams, partners, deadlines, expectations, and the noise of both success and failure. But it won't change you, because you'll carry the strength of this solitude, and the knowledge that you learned to collaborate with yourself first.

And as the last frame of your life fades out, you will enter the void, solo and unseen once again. But it will not matter, because you will have learned to find joy in that state. You will have found yourself. And that is all that matters.

PRINCIPLE

Solitude is the purest collaboration.

PRACTICE

Set a Solo Block—Dedicate two hours this week to creating unseen.

Journal the Voice—Write what emerged from that solitude.

Reframe Loneliness—Replace "lonely" with "alone," and "alone" with "incubating" whenever you feel unseen.

103

OUTPUT: RESILIENCE
AS PRODUCTIVITY

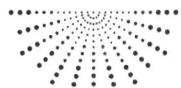

The learnings in this section focus on productivity.

Resilience is releasing in rhythm and sharing work in progress, prov_ng resilience is sometimes about staying in motion.

When you don't get a seat at any table, build your own table.

104

BUILD YOUR OWN ARCHITECTURE

*D*eadlines can be a drug. They may make you sprint or force you to finish, but they also narrow your vision. You rush to meet the clock, not to follow your instinct.

Step back from the calendar, and something unexpected happens: Space opens. Intuition returns. You notice connections. You feel the shape of your own work.

That's when the real architecture begins.

I spent years chasing partnerships, waiting for external validation, thinking someone else's program or platform would be the frame I needed. But every time I handed over my energy, I lost a bit of clarity. I couldn't see which ideas were mine, and which were borrowed.

The turning point came when I held my boundary. I stopped giving away my focus to collaborations that didn't feel right. The result? Freedom. All that energy came back to me, and I could pour it into building my own structures.

This is what resilience looks like in practice: not just saying no to others, but saying yes to the architecture that sustains you.

Every time you invest in your own frameworks—even if they're imperfect, even if they're still in progress—you're building a foundation no one else can take from you.

PRINCIPLE

Resilience is not about chasing deadlines or outsourcing your path. It is about building the architecture that belongs to you.

PRACTICE

Pause the clock: Try a period of working without external deadlines. Let your intuition set the rhythm.

Test the fit: Before saying yes to a partnership, ask: Does this reinforce my architecture, or does it pull me away from it?

Name your structures: Write down the frameworks you're building (projects, methods, series). Each has weight, even in draft form.

Invest inward: When you reclaim time or energy, redirect it into those structures. Don't let it leak away.

Trust attraction: Partnerships worth having will be drawn to what you've built, not demanded from what you've given away.

A lantern that runs on borrowed oil will eventually die out.

REFLECTION

Build your own vessel, fill it with your own flame, and you'll find that others gather around the light.

105

PERMISSION IS NOT THE PRIZE

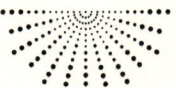

The industry tempts you to chase permission—laurels, grants, greenlights. Those fade, or never even come your way. What endures, and what is possible, is your capacity to create without waiting.

PRINCIPLE

Leverage isn't access; it's what you create when you don't have it.

PRACTICE

Check the source: Does this opportunity give you energy to make, or just optics to show?

Define a no-permission project: What can you make with what you have now (crew of two, one location, modest budget)?

Set a cadence that doesn't need a yes—drafts, scenes, shorts on a rhythm you control.

REFLECTION

Permission is a spark. Journal if you are waiting on that spark from something or someone. Then create that spark yourself. The fire will come.

106

SPLIT THE DAY, SAVE THE FLAME

a solo creator's work splits into two worlds: the generative (making stories, art, film, ideas) and the structural (taxes, finances, systems, logistics). Both are necessary, but they run on different energy. If you let administrative tasks creep into your peak hours, the flame of creation dims. If you ignore admin entirely, the structures collapse beneath your art.

The lantern way is to divide the day with intention. For instance, mornings for creation, afternoons for structure.

PRINCIPLE

Guard your highest energy for the work only you can make. Give your steady energy to the work that sustains what you make.

PRACTICE

Protect the first flame: Commit the first 2–3 hours of your day to creative work. No email, no admin. Only writing, editing, animating, or making.

Build the second scaffold: After lunch, turn to structural work—

taxes, budgets, systems, archiving. Approach it as puzzle-solving, not drudgery.

Close the loop: End each day by writing down the following: One creative win (a scene, a beat, a shot). One structural win (a reconciled number, a filed form, a new system in place).

Weekly balance: At week's end, review both sides: Did the story move forward? Did the foundation strengthen? If both advanced, the lantern stayed lit.

REFLECTION

Art survives not just on inspiration, but on infrastructure. By splitting your day, you save the flame: bright in the morning, steady in the afternoon, and intact by night.

107
RELEASE RHYTHM

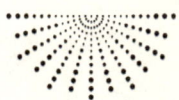

When you hear "release," it's easy to picture the big one: the film premiere, the book launch, the moment when years of work finally hit the world. That's one kind of release—the final release. But waiting only for those climaxes is torture. You starve yourself of feedback, momentum, and the small satisfactions that keep your nervous system alive.

Release is not just an endpoint. It's a rhythm. It's the steady act of letting pieces of your work breathe outside of you—even before they're perfect. A rough animatic. A clip that's "70% there." A storyboard set to music. A short passage shared with a trusted circle.

Each small release is like opening a window in a stuffy room. It doesn't mean the house is finished. It means you can breathe while you keep building.

PRINCIPLE

Release isn't a single moment. It's the practice of sharing your work in stages, so you stay alive to the process while heading toward the finale.

PRACTICE

Define levels of release.

Private: Show your cohort, your partner, or a single peer.

Semi-public: Post a 30-second clip, frame it clearly ("this is a moving storyboard, not final animation").

Public: The completed piece, distributed.

Use small releases as calibration. Feedback helps you see what's working *without* waiting for the end.

Reframe small releases. Don't think of them as "unfinished." Think of them as signals that you're in motion, and as an opportunity to invite connections.

Guard against overexposure. Share enough to breathe, not so much that you burn out watching comments or comparing yourself.

108

SHARE TO SIGNAL

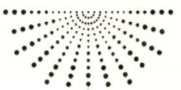

*M*omentum you *show* isn't the same as momentum you *make*. Posting just to quiet your own anxiety may give a brief moment of relief, but it can also backfire—undercutting your reputation or distracting you from the real work.

Instead, share when there's a signal in it—a shot at final quality, a workflow breakthrough, or a piece of process that reflects how you think as a filmmaker. LinkedIn, in particular, is for signals—things that represent you to the industry at large. Save the raw experiments for private rooms or casual socials.

PRINCIPLE

Anxiety isn't a strategy. Design your release so it says what you want it to say.

PRACTICE

Before you share, ask:

Am I posting to *soothe* my fear of invisibility?

Or am I posting to *signal* something real—skill, clarity, direction?

If it's the first, sit on it. If it's the second, frame it clearly, release it, and let it work for you.

109

FINISH TO LEARN

*R*esilience in creative work isn't about collecting endless skills. It's about learning *just enough* to finish something—and letting the finished work itself become the teacher.

Too many artists, myself included, get caught in the trap of thinking we have to "catch up" to everyone who's been doing this longer. We binge tutorials, sign up for classes, and dive into tool after tool. The result is we know *a lot about* the work but have little actually finished. And nothing undermines resilience faster than the feeling of always learning and never arriving.

You don't need twenty years of experience in every discipline you touch. You only need enough to carry a project across the finish line. Every time you do, you expand your range. The finished piece teaches you more than another lecture or another tutorial ever will.

PRINCIPLE

Resilience comes from releasing the burden of mastery, and returning to the discipline of *completion*.

PRACTICE

Anchor learning to a project. Don't just dive into Unreal or Nuke or Resolve "just to learn." Decide: What shot, what scene, what sequence am I making that requires this skill? Then learn only what that shot demands.

Use the 70% Rule. Stop polishing at "good enough for this project." Ship it. Archive it. Move on. Learning multiplies across projects, not inside one perfect attempt. Are there exceptions to this rule?

Yes.

For instance, I recently decided to do the sound design for one of my films. I did focus on achieving a level of perfection here but not for its own sake. Instead, I used that drive for perfection to help me build out and organize my sound library inventory, and my expertise in using the variety of toolsets to do sound design. This is an investment in my workflow and pipeline that will apply to all projects moving forward and help me deliver the audio portion of my projects at a high quality.

Define your baseline and your areas of expertise. Baseline = the minimum competence to carry a project to completion (edit, render, color, basic animation). Areas of expertise = the 1–2 areas you can go deep *only if your current project demands it.*

Close the loop fast. Every new technique must show up in a finished render, a finished page, or a finished shot within days, not months. Otherwise it's just theory.

REFLECTION

You will always feel behind. You will always feel others know more. The truth: Resilience doesn't require you to match their years. It requires you to *finish what's yours.*

Your lantern is not a library. It's a light that moves with you, one finished step at a time.

110

LEARNING BY DOING

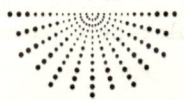

*L*earning feels safe; doing feels risky.

Learning: You can stay abstract. There's no stake. You watch a video, absorb, and it feels like progress.

Doing: Suddenly your work is on trial—by your own standards most of all. Every imperfect output feels like a verdict, even if it's just iteration.

For the longest time, I allowed myself to stay in the safe space of learning. I am a lifelong student, there's no doubt about that, and there's no issue with that.

The problem was that I skipped the doing. I minimized it. I deferred it. I filled up my schedule with "learning opportunities" to avoid the doing.

The thing is, knowledge without practice is a lantern left unlit. Learning can spark curiosity, but only doing creates fire.

PRINCIPLE

The creative life rewards those who step from theory into practice, even if the first steps feel awkward and unfinished.

PRACTICE

Test immediately: Each time you learn something new, spend at least two minutes applying it. Don't wait for the "right" project. A small, disposable test is enough to light the lantern.

Separate labs from work: Keep a "Playground Project" where the only goal is experiments. Ugly is expected. The point is iteration, not polish.

Count iterations, not masterpieces: Success isn't finishing a perfect shot—it's running another test. Progress comes from stacking experiments, not chasing flawless outcomes.

Record the flame: At the end of each session, write one sentence: *"Today I tested ___."* That simple act shifts the reward from imagined perfection to real practice.

REFLECTION

Learning feels safe because it offers instant closure. Doing feels harsh because it exposes imperfection. By redefining "doing" as testing—not proving—you bring the same reward loop into your practice.

This is transformation of learning into a form that'll serve you well. Each test is a step forward, each step a flicker of light. Over time, those flickers add up to a flame bright enough to finish your project.

What are you doing right now that is keeping you in a safe space instead of "making" art?

111

STACK OR SPIKE

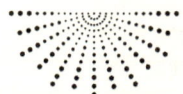

For solo creators, resilience begins with awareness. Awareness of the different tracks pulling on you—creating, releasing, promoting. Awareness of the ways each path stresses your system. Awareness that you can't do it all at once.

That's where the choice comes in: Do you keep walking and leave steady lights behind, or do you stop and light a fire big enough to be seen from far away?

Stacking means *producing and releasing* without heavy promotion. You finish the project, put it out, and keep going. Each release is like placing a lantern on the path—a quiet light that continues to work for you.

In practice: publish a course to Udemy, upload a short film to YouTube, release a book to Amazon, make a single thoughtful LinkedIn post. Quiet marketing like SEO or platform searches keeps those lanterns glowing long after you've moved on.

Spiking means *marketing and amplifying* one project with focus. You stop walking, gather your resources, and build a bonfire. This takes more energy, but it shines brighter and draws attention.

In practice: plan a launch campaign, cut trailers, write a newsletter series, partner for promotion, maybe even invest in ads. One project gets your full push.

Resilience for solo creators means knowing you can't spike everything. If you try, you'll burn out. But if you only stack, your work risks being overlooked.

The discipline is in awareness: recognizing which mode you're in, naming it, and accepting the tradeoffs. Most of the time, stack—finish, release, leave lanterns behind you. Occasionally, spike—build the bonfire that signals your presence to the wider world.

Resilience is not just endurance. It's the awareness to choose your mode, the grit to keep stacking, and the courage to spike when it matters.

112

ALCHEMY: RESILIENCE
AS TRANSFORMATION

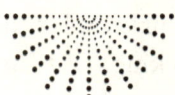

*I*n this section, we look at how resilience relates to the very powerful process and act of transformation.

Turning hardship, failure, or endings into strength, insight, and new light is, in my mind, one of the best ways to build your resilience.

HARVEST THE LAST LIGHT

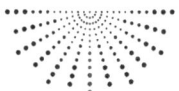

*E*very experience has a closing chapter. When you know you're near the end of something, don't drift away—lean in harder.

Use those last moments to test your growth, sharpen your discernment, and take everything you can from the light before it fades. That harvest becomes fuel for your next journey.

REFLECTION

Have you ever journaled about the experience of a project right as it ended? Often you are too tired to do it, but that fresh capture can be a source of much learning when you come back to it over time.

TEA, COFFEE, BEER, WHISKEY

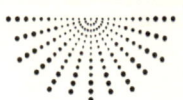

*E*very filmmaker picks a fuel. Some run on coffee—grinding through late nights, jittery but relentless. Others choose tea —calmer, slower, reflective, deliberate. Some turn to beer—networking, hanging out, hoping social lubrication will turn into opportunity. And a few end up at whiskey—the harder stuff, where the edges blur and the coping strategies cut deeper.

All of these have their place. Coffee powers the hustle. Tea fosters thoughtfulness. Beer connects you with others. Whiskey numbs the pain for a while. But none of them are sustainable.

At the end of the day, there's only one thing you truly need: water. Water is health, clarity, and the only fuel that sustains you long enough to finish the film and keep the lantern lit.

PRINCIPLE

Pick the right fuel. Know that water sustains.

PRACTICE

Track your fuel Notice what you reach for when stressed.

    Swap once: Replace one stimulant with water this week.

    Morning ritual: Begin one day with water before anything else.

WISDOM OF NAPS

*Y*ou don't only learn while awake. The brain processes, organizes, and strengthens new knowledge during sleep.

A nap is not wasted time—it is part of the work. Sleep consolidates learning, connects patterns, and primes insight. Naps are not retreat—they are rehearsal for breakthrough.

PRINCIPLE

In creative work, rest is not absence. It is part of the rhythm that keeps the lantern lit.

PRACTICE

Rest cadence: Set a weekly rhythm: a nap window, a daily walk, a water-drinking target.

SUNSHINE AND WALKS

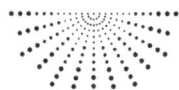

*T*ake a walk. Early morning, 20 minutes, sunshine on your face. Reflect, contemplate, strategize—or don't think at all. Just walk. Notice the leaves, the insects, the life all around you. Remember: If humanity found the same insect on Mars, the world would erupt in joy. Here on Earth, it's a miracle we take for granted.

This is your moment. You walk alone, but you're not alone. The sun is shining on you. The ground beneath your feet is a massive ball of energy spinning through space, carrying you, supporting you, sustaining you. In that walk, you touch stories untold, you shine a lantern on the lives around you.

A 20-minute walk restores clarity. To notice leaves, insects, the ordinary miracles around you is to remember life's scale. You walk alone, but are never alone.

The lantern is lit anew.

PRINCIPLE

Walks rekindle the lantern.

PRACTICE

Daily step: Commit to one short walk this week.

Notice one miracle: On your walk, think about one overlooked detail of your life.

Return with light: After the walk, ask: What did this clarify for me?

117

TURN SHIT INTO GOLD

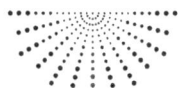

*E*very creative path collects its share of waste—broken collaborations, false promises, time lost. The instinct is to carry bitterness, but bitterness is just dead weight. The lantern way is transmutation: Refine the mess into principle, clarity, or craft. Gold is not just the prize at the end. Gold is what you make from what should have ruined you.

Let's take this book as an example.

This book is itself an act of turning shit into gold. Along my journey, I have faced moments that became anger, resentment, or regret. It took a lot of work, but I shaped them into principles for myself. These Lantern Learnings I am sharing with you are not abstract wisdom; they are lived struggles transmuted into light that has steadied me, clarified my feelings, and given me language to continue.

PRINCIPLE

The challenges will not end. They will return in new shapes, at new scales. But each time, remember the darkness is not the end. And the act of carrying light through it is the gold.

PRACTICE

Name the Waste

Write down the moment that still stings—the project that collapsed, the betrayal, the rejection, the wasted hours. Don't dress it up. Name it plainly.

Extract the Principle

Ask: *What did this reveal to me about people, about process, about myself?* Distill one sentence of truth. ("No is a full sentence." "Fit matters more than urgency." "My peace is worth more than access.")

Carry It Forward

Turn that sentence into a lantern. Keep it visible—in your notebook, on your wall, in your daily practice. The principle becomes the gold, and the bitterness is left behind.

REFLECTION

Everyone has mess in their life. The ones who last refine it and turn it into gold. Don't carry waste—carry gold.

118

STOP THE REPLAY

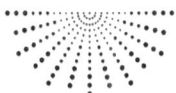

*T*he mind replays unresolved interactions—a conversation that cut too deep, a silence that stung, a moment where you may have hurt someone or been hurt yourself. These loops return because the ego craves closure.

Principle

Resilience isn't about suppressing these loops. It's about facing them long enough to take what's useful—then releasing the rest.

Practice

Catch the loop: Notice when your mind starts rerunning the same scene. Say aloud: *This is a replay, not reality.*

Name the pull: Ask, *Am I wanting retaliation, repair, or release?* Only the last two move you forward.

Extract the signal: Beneath the sting is usually a truth: "I want acknowledgment." "I mishandled that moment." "I need firmer boundaries." Write it down.

Choose the Path:

Art—Channel the insight into your craft.

Healing—If it only reopens wounds, don't force it into art. Seek therapy, ritual, or rest.

Repair—If grace can close the loop with the other person, consider it.

Release—Once the lesson, repair, or art is made, let the loop end. Don't keep carrying what has already taught you.

Guardrail:

Not every replay deserves redemption. Some need nothing more than to be acknowledged and left behind.

119

AIM YOUR OBSESSION RIGHT

*I*nstead of burning energy on loops about people or events you can't control, resilience comes from training that same obsessive energy onto your craft, where every replay makes the work sharper.

PRINCIPLE

Obsession is not the enemy. The mind already knows how to replay, refine, and fixate—it's just often hooked on the wrong reel.

PRACTICE

Catch the hook: When you notice yourself obsessing over someone else's words or actions, say: *This is fuel. I can redirect it.*

Swap the reel: Open Final Draft, pick one scene, and let your mind replay *that* moment with the same intensity.

Walk it out: On your daily walk, consciously shift the mental loop. Instead of replaying a sting, replay your character's dilemma, or your camera movement, until it feels lived-in.

Keep a ledger: Each time you notice outside-world obsession, log it. Then log the scene, beat, or project you transmuted it into. Watch the ledger fill with pages instead of replays.

Guardrail

Don't mistake suppression for redirection. First acknowledge the sting, then turn the energy toward creation.

120

AMBITION WITHOUT ATTACHMENT

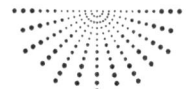

*W*hen ambition is tied to comparison, judgment, or internet applause, it mutates into something corrosive. You end up measuring your worth not by your practice but by the noise around it.

WHY IT MATTERS

You will always have peers who rise faster, louder, flashier.

You will always have critics (or "haters") who cut down what you make.

You cannot escape these forces—but you can decide how much they get to define you.

Without boundaries, ambition collapses into shame: *"I should be further by now. I should be like them."*

With practice, ambition becomes fuel: *"I will keep walking my path. My next step is enough."*

PRINCIPLE

Ambition is not the enemy. The desire to do more, to reach higher, to make better work—that hunger is what keeps your flame alive.

PRACTICE

Separate flame from feedback: Remember, applause and criticism both belong to the crowd. Your flame belongs to you. Don't confuse the two.

Anchor in the work: Instead of asking, *"Did they like it?"* ask, *"Did I finish it? Did I give it truth?"* That is the measure only you can control.

Expect the punch: When you read reviews, prepare for the dopamine rollercoaster. Don't fight it. Note it: *"That was a hit. That was a sting."* Awareness is half the armor.

Reframe the hater: Each critic proves your work reached beyond your safe circle. Even a negative comment means your art traveled. That's progress.

Keep ambition as blessing: Wanting more does not mean you are failing now. It means you are alive to the possibility of growth. Hold ambition without chaining your worth to it.

REFLECTION

A film's success—or failure—is never yours alone. It's a collaboration. But your resilience, your practice, your peace? Those are yours to own fully. Let ambition push you forward, but don't let judgment—from the outside or the inside—drag you down.

121

WALKING THROUGH FAILURE

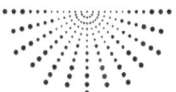

ailure feels final in the moment—the late night, the shaky delivery, the comparison to someone brilliant. But the lantern way is not to deny the sting. It's to move through it step by step, until the sting becomes fuel.

The Stages of Recovery

Despair – "I'll never be at their level." The first wave hits hard. Let it. Don't rush to reframe. Acknowledge the collapse.

Recognition – "But I learned something I can't unlearn." Even in failure, some thread of clarity shows up. Name it. That's the seed.

Orientation – "This is where my compass points." Re-center on your lane—the crafts that are truly yours. Failure in one space often reveals where you belong in another.

Renewal – "I may not pass this, but I can deepen where I'm strongest." Turn the lesson sideways. How does it sharpen your true path?

Motion – "Now go make the next thing." Carry the clarity forward in a concrete step—one shot, one page, one scene.

PRINCIPLE

Failure isn't the opposite of resilience; it's the doorway to it.

PRACTICE

Name the sting: Write down the exact sentence your mind is saying ("I'll never be at their level"). Read it back. See it as thought, not truth.

Extract the thread: Note one thing you learned in failing—even if it hurts. That's your takeaway.

Re-center: Write your role in two sentences. Does this failure change it, or confirm it?

Take one step: Choose the smallest next creative action you can actually finish in a day.

HARVEST, RELEASE, MOVE ON

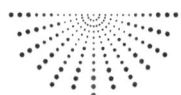

*C*riticism will come. Sometimes harsh, sometimes dismissive, sometimes fair. The mistake is not in receiving it—the mistake is in carrying it. When you let someone else's words live rent-free in your mind, they steal energy that belongs to your craft, your loved ones, and your peace.

Your task is not to fight every critic, nor to prove them wrong. Your task is to harvest what is useful, release what is not, and move on.

PRINCIPLE

Presence is your fuel. Entanglement is the drag.

PRACTICE

Harvest the lesson: Ask, "Is there one thing here I can use to get better?" Take that seed—and only that.

Release the rest: Say aloud, "This belongs to them, not me." You don't need to carry what isn't yours.

Anchor back to work: Bring your attention to the smallest next thing you can do well: a line of dialogue, a frame of light, a brush-stroke of color. Action clears mental noise.

Move on: Your worth isn't measured by a review. It's measured by your ability to keep going, to keep making.

REFLECTION

Every artist is tempted to replay slights and criticisms, but the truth is that even the most celebrated creators live with detractors. The day you stop receiving criticism is the day your work stops reaching anyone.

123

THE WARRIOR ARTIST

*E*very artist must decide who they are when the world wounds them. Some see themselves as fragile, craving acceptance. Others choose to walk as warrior artists. A warrior artist expects wounds—from critics, from rejection, from their own missteps. But they do not let those wounds define them.

PRINCIPLE

A warrior artist tends to what must be healed, carries what must be carried, and keeps moving. Their inner resilience is not up for negotiation.

PRACTICE

Write your creed: Put into words the stance you want to carry through your creative life. What do you expect? What do you refuse to yield?

Expect the wound: When criticism or rejection comes, remind yourself: *"This was always part of the path. I trained for this."*

Tend and move: Heal what must be healed, but do not stop. A warrior artist keeps momentum.

Protect the core: Your work can be judged, praised, or dismissed, but your inner identity is yours alone.

You cannot choose whether you will be wounded. You can only choose whether you will keep walking. A creed makes the choice in advance.

124

A FILMMAKER'S CREED

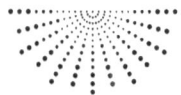

I am a warrior artist.
    I do not walk this path expecting ease.
I expect wounds—
from critics, from rejection,
from betrayal, from my own mistakes.
I expect wounds. I expect setbacks.
They will not stop me.
They will not define me.
They will not touch the core of who I am.
My inner flame, my inner resilience, my inner identity.
I will tend to the cuts, carry the scars, and keep moving.
Because my flame does not come from the world's applause.
It comes from the practice of showing up, again and again.
I am not here to be coddled, or to beg for acceptance.
I am here to make. To keep making.
My creed is simple:
Endure the wound.
Protect my core.
Keep moving.

Reflection

Every artist must find their own creed—a few words they can return to when the noise rises, when rejection stings, when doubt circles close.

The creed above is mine.

What is yours? Don't have one? Write it for yourself.

125

DIRECTION OVER PERFECTION

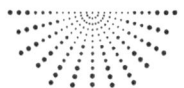

*E*very crossroads tempts you with hesitation. *Is this the right project? The right publisher? The right timing?* You can waste months testing the wind, waiting for certainty. But certainty rarely comes. What moves you forward is not perfection, but direction.

Choose a direction. Even if it's not flawless, it gives you a line to walk. Once you're moving, you can adjust your pace, refine your tools, and course-correct. But standing still in search of the "perfect" option moves you nowhere.

PRINCIPLE

Progress beats perfection every time. A clear direction, even imperfect, creates momentum. Momentum creates clarity.

REFLECTION

What small step today will move me one step down my chosen road?

If I let go of the need for perfect choice, what would I do next?

The lantern doesn't reveal the whole path. It only shows the next few steps. Trust that moving forward, imperfectly but deliberately, is what lights the way.

126

MARK PROGRESS

*P*erfection is a mirage—you never arrive, you only move toward it endlessly. What you can touch, what you can trust, is *progress*. Progress is the proof you're alive in your work. Without marking it, the journey feels like wandering in circles.

WHY IT MATTERS

When you only measure yourself against the "big break" or the "finished masterpiece," you erase the hundreds of steps that got you there.

Without reflection, you forget how much ground you've covered. You think you're stuck when, in truth, you're miles ahead of where you started.

PRINCIPLE

Progress is fuel: Seeing your own momentum builds the resilience to keep going.

PRACTICE

Daily marker: At the end of the day, write one line, *"Today I..."* followed by one concrete action you completed (wrote a page, made a call, learned a shortcut, set a boundary).

Weekly reflection: Every week, look back and make a list of *five wins*, no matter how small. Notice the pattern: You are moving.

Monthly checkpoint: Once a month, create a short "progress report" for yourself. Summarize what you started, what you advanced, and what you closed. Keep it in one folder as your lantern archive.

Celebrate forward, not finished: When you share with others, share progress, not perfection. "Here's what I worked through this week" is more authentic than pretending you've already arrived.

Anchor with gratitude: Close each reflection by naming one thing you're grateful for in your process. Gratitude locks in progress as meaning, not just motion.

YOU ARE ENOUGH

*A*t the end of it all, resilience is not about proving your strength to the world. It is about proving steadiness to yourself.

There will be days when you keep going, even without applause. Days when you let go of a project, not in defeat, but in discernment. Days when you carry the weight of rejection or rupture longer than others—and still, eventually, turn it into fuel.

If you remember nothing else from this book, remember this: Your lantern is not powered by circumstance. It is powered by the small, steady choices you make to keep the flame alive—a thread of curiosity, a breath of grace, a spark of generosity.

Resilience is not firework light. It is lantern light—fragile, ordinary, easily overlooked. And yet, when carried through the dark, it is enough.

You are enough.

TURNING INSIGHT INTO ACTION

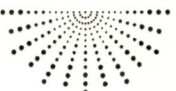

By now you've read the Lantern Learnings, and you understand its principles. But understanding alone won't change your life. Practice will.

Here's how to ground these ideas so they don't just stay on the page:

1. Pause.

When a situation stirs you—frustration, fear, doubt—stop for a moment. Take a breath. Notice what's happening.

2. Name.

Identify which Lantern applies. Is this about boundaries, resilience, or focus? Naming gives you clarity.

3. Apply.

Choose one practice. Keep it small. Repeat it. Don't wait for the perfect moment—apply it in the messy one you're in.

4. Reflect.

At the end of the day or week, ask: Did this situation shift how I acted? How I felt? Reflection locks the learning in.

5. Repeat.

These are not one-time lessons. They're habits you return to, over and over, until they become part of how you move through the world.

Think of this book less as something you finish, and more as something you carry.

These Lantern Learnings aren't instructions to memorize. They're reminders you revisit—when you falter, when you're uncertain, when you need a light.

A reminder to *make* instead of worrying if you'll *make it*.

EPILOGUE: THE
LANTERN'S FLAME

*Y*ou've carried these pages to the end, but the real work begins outside of them. The lantern isn't mine to hold anymore—it's yours.

Take it into the places that matter most—the conversations where silence feels heavy, the mornings where doubt lingers, the nights when the next step looks unclear. Let one principle, one practice be enough to keep you moving.

You don't need to master all of this at once. You don't need to prepare for every possibility or every mistake. What matters is the response you choose, the grace you return to, and the resilience you build.

If you forget, return. If you falter, return. If you lose your way, return. That's what the lantern is for.

Not to light the whole path. Just to give you enough to take the next step.

Every principle in these pages is only a bit of light to carry you a little further. Like Prospero at the end of *The Tempest*, I know that all our "charms"—the techniques, the craft, the strategies—can only go so far. In the end, what strength we have is our own: faint, but steady.

Art is never certain. The road bends, the weather shifts, the audience forgets. But the lantern is not about certainty. It is about enough light for the next step.

So carry it with you—in solitude and in company, in failure and in small victories. And when your flame feels faint, remember that even the smallest light still breaks the dark.

Writing this book has been its own lantern for me. Every lesson here was born not from theory but from lived experience—from reflection, therapy, mistakes, and the hard work of shaping pain into practice. I haven't conquered any of it, nor is that the goal. Feeling deeply is part of the life I chose as an artist. It isn't something I want to numb; it's something I need to steward, so that my family and my work can receive the best version of me.

That's why these pages exist. Not as a declaration of mastery, but as a process I can return to whenever I stumble, as I surely will. Resilience isn't a finish line; it's a rhythm. My hope is that when your path darkens, you might find in these words a moment of relief, a fragment of direction, or a practice to steady your own flame.

The lantern is lit. Now go make the next thing.

LANTERN WORKSHEET

Lantern Line
>My lantern exists to:
>**Grace + Boundaries**
>Two acts of generosity I'll offer freely this week/month/quarter/year
>1.
>2.
>One boundary I'll hold this week/month/quarter/year

Role + Frame
>My two-sentence role statement

Three proof artifacts that support my role statement:
>1.
>2.
>3.

Signal Over Noise
>My one piece to finish this week/month (remember: it must move five strangers)

How does this piece work for me? Look at these prompts below to answer.
>Aligns with craft/lane?
>Serves growth/audience?
>Protects peace/principles?

Curate the Scene

Three Rooms/Events I'll return to over the next 3/6/9/12 months

1)

2)

3)

Threshold for Public Statements/Social Media Posts

My five checks:

True?

Aligned?

Supports my Filmmaker's (or chosen vocation's) voice?

Helps someone specific?

Am I ready to evaluate and accept risk to my family/friends/colleagues?

Identify my Partners

Sacred partner (and why they matter)

1)

2)

Hustle partner (scope/limits)

1)

2)

3)

Fuel & Rest

Coffee? Or Walks?

Naps? Or Gym?

Water?

LANTERN WORKSHEET (SAMPLE)

Lantern Line

My lantern exists to: create entertainment that holds meaning to me

Grace + Boundaries

Two acts of generosity I'll offer freely this week/month/quarter/year

1. Offer notes on a fellow artist's creative project
2. Volunteer on a non-profit drama club project

One boundary I'll hold this week/month/quarter/year

- Decline (or redirect appropriately) colleagues reaching out with unrelated tech emergencies

Role + Frame

My two-sentence role statement

I'm a filmmaker, storyteller, and educator working at the leading edge of cinema and technology.

Three proof artifacts that support my role statement:

1. My films are available on streaming platforms.
2. My scripts have placed in several screenwriting contests.

3. I am an Unreal Engine Authorized Instructor (Gold) with a focus on Real Time and Virtual Production for filmmakers

Signal Over Noise

My one piece to finish this week/month (remember: it must move five strangers)

Complete LOVE LOVE: Fractures – an anthology of my short films that I must deliver to a distributor in Q4 2025.

How does this piece work for me? Look at these prompts below to answer.

Aligns with craft/lane? Yes. Aligns with my role as a writer-filmmaker and technology craftsperson.

Serves growth/audience? Yes. Builds on my thematic franchise of LOVE LOVE, that I'm building as an umbrella for several of my projects.

Protects peace/principles? Yes. Gives me peace to know that the work of all the artists involved in these films will be available to the world at the highest quality I can deliver within my means.

Curate the Scene

Three Rooms/Events I'll return to over the next 3/6/9/12 months
1) Unreal Fest. This is a commitment for me to build expertise.
2) Filmmaker Group. A monthly group meetup of peers.
3) Family events. I will prioritize events with family in 2026.

Threshold for Public Statements/Social Media Posts

My five checks:
True?
Aligned?
Supports my Filmmaker's (or chosen vocation's) voice?
Helps someone specific?
Am I ready to evaluate and accept risk to my family/friends/colleagues?

My social media has been focused mainly on my films and work, and very rare personal statements on world events (despite any backlash, as my integrity is as important to me as my career might be).

Identify my Partners

Sacred partner (and why they matter)

1) My wife, mother of our children. She makes everything possible.

2) (private)

Hustle partner (scope/limits)

1) (private)

2) (private)

Fuel & Rest

Coffee? Or Walks? Currently both. Walks are consistent/daily.

Naps? Or Gym? Kickboxing workouts are my only focus.

Water? I brought a reusable bottle, but training myself to fill it and use it.

MONTHLY PROGRESS
REPORT WORKSHEET

Mark Progress. Not Perfection.

Month:
    Project(s):

Key Wins

List 5 things you accomplished this month—big or small, finished or unfinished.

∿

∿

∿

∿

∿

Steps Taken

Write down concrete actions that moved you forward. (e.g., "outlined Act 2," "sent email to X," "edited one sequence").

Lessons Learned

Note what you discovered about your process, your craft, or yourself.

Boundaries & Breakthroughs

Where did you protect your energy, say no, or shift course in a way that created clarity?

Next Steps

List 3 priorities for the next month—realistic, clear actions.

Gratitude Anchor

End with one sentence of gratitude for your own effort this month: "I'm grateful that I..."

Tip: keep each month's report in a single folder or notebook. Over time, you'll have a living archive of your creative journey—proof of progress even when completion feels far away.

MONTHLY PROGRESS REPORT
WORKSHEET (SAMPLE)

Mark Progress. Not Perfection.

Month: November 2025
   Project(s): LOVE LOVE: Fractures

Key Wins
   List 5 things you accomplished this month—big or small, finished or unfinished.
   • Built up my Sound Design libraries for use in current and future projects
   • Organized all the libraries so that they can be managed and used effectively
   • Prepared all the nine short films for release by adding in licensed sound effects from purchased libraries to avoid expense of licensing original music
   • Learned and implemented several audio/dialogue cleaning techniques using iZOTOPE plugins and avoided ADR work
   • Started brainstorming on the Poster and Synopsis for the film

Steps Taken

Write down concrete actions that moved you forward. (e.g., "outlined Act 2," "sent email to X," "edited one sequence").

- Shared several of the short films with colleagues to get feedback and notes
- Researched all the channels/streamers I'm interested in to ensure the film will meet their requirements

Lessons Learned

Note what you discovered about your process, your craft, or yourself.

- I learned that revisiting old material can be fruitful, but only if you ensure it's adding more value than just itself. For instance, when I revisit an old film, I'm not only improving the film, but I'm building out my entire infrastructure that'll help me make my *next* film. *So I didn't just edit my old short films into an anthology. I built my own architecture for my future films!*
- As a storyteller, I've learned that I must slow down and set up the world in greater detail than I personally need, so that I can take everyone else along with me on the journey the story seeks to deliver.

Boundaries & Breakthroughs

Where did you protect your energy, say no, or shift course in a way that created clarity?

- I declined invites to parties and networking opportunities. My new approach is to network through work. I'd rather do projects with people than hang around in a bar drinking beer and talking about doing projects with them.
- I deflected asks for tech support as I do not want to be known as the "go to" guy for such questions. These come in fast and furious, and often with urgency, and can upset my entire flow.

Next Steps

List 3 priorities for the next month—realistic, clear actions.

- Submit my finished film and all supporting marketing collateral to the distributor
- Return focus to the new film project and develop it for production in 2026
- Deliver an update to my Udemy course on Making Metahumans Playable to address all the updates made in the latest Unreal Engine version.

Gratitude Anchor

End with one sentence of gratitude for your own effort this month:
"I'm grateful that I..."

I am grateful that I had the courage and intuition to start on this film project when everyone told me I should not. I am also grateful for their input, as it helped me realize that it was not the film project I was after, but it was all the workflow improvements I'd put into place, and all the learnings I'd get. I know now that without those, my next film would have suffered. And now, with those in place, it'll add to the quality and efficiencies of production for my next film project.

ABOUT THE AUTHOR

Nikhil Kamkolkar is a writer–director and **Unreal Authorized Instructor (Gold)** focused on screenplay development and real-time/virtual production—spanning previsualization (previs) through final pixels in ICVFX. An **Unreal Engine Animation Fellowship** alum, he is in pre-production on a sci-fi feature film that integrates Unreal with emerging AI/ICVFX workflows.

His debut feature rom-com **LOVE LOVE** is streaming globally on Amazon Prime, HOOPLA, etc. His anthology of award-winning shorts titled **LOVE LOVE: Fractures** is in post-production. His TV pilots (sci-fi, horror, thriller) have placed in **Screencraft** and **Final Draft Big Break**.

Alongside filmmaking, he's held roles at **Microsoft, MTV, Nickelodeon,** and **Topic**. Several of his screenplays are published as books on major retailers. His non-fiction writing focuses on film-maker practice & creative resilience.

Based in New Jersey, Nikhil Kamkolkar works internationally.

More at **KAM9.TV**.

instagram.com/nikhilnyc
facebook.com/nikhilkamkolkar
tiktok.com/@kam9tv

ALSO BY NIKHIL KAMKOLKAR

LOVE LOVE: Screenplay by Nikhil Kamkolkar (Rising Stakes Screenplay Series)

Short Film Scripts: By Nikhil Kamkolkar (Rising Stakes Screenplay Series)

RAW Deception: Novelization of a screenplay (Rising Stakes Screenplay Series)

LOVE LOVE: From Fantasy to Forever (Film)

Streaming on Amazon Prime, HOOPLA, and more.

LOVE LOVE: Fractures (Anthology Feature Film)

Coming Soon

∼

LEAVE A REVIEW

If this book helped, a short honest review really helps other creators discover it. Thank you.

∼

www.ingramcontent.com/pod-product-compliance
Lightning Source LLC
Chambersburg PA
CBHW021223130626
46554CB00004B/1336